Soul Feast

Marjorie J. Thompson

Soul Feast

An Invitation to the
Christian Spiritual Life

 Westminster John Knox Press
Louisville, Kentucky

Unless otherwise noted, all scripture quotations are from the New Revised Standard Version of the Bible, copyright © 1989 by the Division of Christian Education of the National Council of the Churches of Christ in the U.S.A., and are used by permission.

Book design by Drew Stevens
Cover design by Tanya R. Hahn
Illustrations by Cecilia Amorocho

First edition

Published by Westminster John Knox Press
Louisville, Kentucky

This book is printed on acid-free paper that meets the American National Standards Institute Z39.48 standard. ∞

PRINTED IN THE UNITED STATES OF AMERICA

99 00 01 02 03 04 — 10 9 8

Library of Congress Cataloging-in-Publication Data

Thompson, Marjorie J., date.
    Soul feast : an invitation to the Christian spiritual life /
Marjorie J. Thompson.—1st ed.
        p.   cm.
    Includes bibliographical references.
    ISBN 0-664-25548-5 (alk. paper)
    1. Spiritual life—Christianity.   I. Title.
BV4501.2.T495   1995
248—dc20   95-5098

To John,

my dearest companion on the journey
and my intimate friend
at the Table

My soul is satisfied as with a rich feast,
and my mouth praises you with joyful lips . . .
                                    —Psalm 63:5

Contents

Contents

Foreword

It is a real honour and joy for me to write this foreword to
Marjorie Thompson's book *Soul Feast, An Invitation to the Christian
Spiritual Life*, especially because of our long friendship and my
great admiration for her person and her work. I met Marjorie for
the first time in the fall of 1979 while I was on the faculty of Yale
Divinity School. After having received her master's degree at
McCormick Theological Seminary in Chicago, Marjorie came
to Yale to focus her studies on ecumenical Christian spirituality
and to become more familiar with its different practices and disciplines. Very soon I became aware that Marjorie had unique gifts
of mind and heart that enabled her to make significant contri-
butions to the spiritual life of the Christian church. Her personality, which loves order and clarity, her Presbyterian tradition
that highly values the spoken and written word, and her conviction that all churches need a deeper spiritual vision enabled
her to accomplish much during her time at Yale. She read
widely, spoke with many people, and visited a rich variety of
retreat and conference centres. After finishing her year at Yale, she
joined the staff of a large East Coast Presbyterian church and
developed there a fruitful ministry with a special emphasis on spiritual formation. When Marjorie moved to Nashville, Tennessee,
almost four years later, she was well prepared to broaden and
deepen her spiritual ministry through teaching, workshops, and
retreats.

   This book is the fruit of Marjorie's personal practice, her
solid studies, and long experience in spiritual formation. It
brings together in a clear, concise way the essence of her ministry. There are few books in which a solid biblical vision and a
practical, hands-on approach are so well integrated. When you
have read and lived this book, you have been in touch with the

best that Christian spirituality has to offer. Marjorie's treatment of spiritual reading, praying, worship, fasting, examination of conscience, spiritual guidance, hospitality, and the development of a "rule of life," makes the spiritual life readily accessible to people from many different walks of life.

As I went through the pages of this book, I could feel the strong yet gentle guidance of its author. Marjorie is clear, specific, and direct, but she does not impose, push, or manipulate. She simply invites us to create the space where the life of God in us can be nurtured and brought to fruition.

Our busy lives make it hard for us to create free time or space for God. In fact, as Spinoza says, there is a "horror vacui," a fear of empty space. *Soul Feast* shows us that the disciplines of the spiritual life are meant to offer creative boundaries to that empty space within and among us, so that we can acknowledge it without fear and allow God to transform there our stony hearts into hearts of flesh. Spiritual disciplines are nothing more and nothing less than ways to create a room where Christ can invite us to feast with him at the table of abundance.

One of the most encouraging qualities of this book is its ecumenicity. The language is inclusive of all Christians. It is a book that will speak to those who sincerely seek God, irrespective of denomination or tradition. Marjorie's invitation to the spiritual life is a beautiful affirmation of the truth that, beyond dogmatic and liturgical differences, there is a place where we can experience the common Source of our sustenance. It is a place where the Spirit of Jesus wants to dwell and lead us to the freedom of the children of God.

I am convinced that for those who take this book seriously and apply it to their individual as well as communal lives, a true transformation will take place—a transformation that will affect not only their interior life but also the life of the Body of Christ, the Church.

HENRI J. M. NOUWEN

Acknowledgments

I wish to thank the Theology and Worship Unit of the Presbyterian Church (U.S.A.) for asking me to join in the initial project, developing a written resource on Christian spirituality for beginners. In particular, I am grateful to Dick Junkin for extending the invitation through the unit's Office of Discipleship and Spirituality. My fond thanks to Carol Wehrheim for working with Dick and me to discern the direction and shape this resource should take and for asking me to be its author. Jeanette Hardy has supplied able administrative help from the office in Louisville.

It is an unusual privilege and unimaginable help for an author to have the benefit of eight readers to advise and guide the development of a book manuscript. This extraordinary benefit was provided by the Office of Discipleship and Spirituality under Dick's direction. My profound gratitude and blessing to Ben Campbell Johnson, Dick Junkin, Martha Jane Petersen, Loretta Ross-Gotta, Carson Salyer, Carol Wehrheim, and Ann Young, who read volumes of rough draft pages, met with me twice, and responded to my work-in-progress with insight, clarity, challenge, support, and encouragement. I am deeply indebted also to Dr. Anne Wimberly of the Interdenominational Theological Center in Atlanta for taking time to read the early draft and offer valuable insights and resources from an African-American perspective. I am grateful for encouragement received along the way from Howard Rice, Ted Yaple, and Glenn Hinson.

Perhaps no other single person has exerted a more profound influence on the direction of my spiritual life than Henri Nouwen. Were it not for Henri's insight, encouragement, and support, I would not have the background to write a book such as this. Neither would I have met the man who most fully embodies the continued stretching and support of my spiritual life, with whom I share the vocation of Christian marriage. I am grateful beyond words for Henri's faithful friendship and for the gift of his foreword to this book.

Of course, this work could not have been completed without the quiet and patient support of my husband, John Mogabgab. Not only did he take up the burden of many household tasks and suffer countless hours of imposed solitude while I wrote, but he generously gave his time to coach me on the mysteries of computer logic and read the entire manuscript to assure me of its value. I trust his judgment.

My thanks to all who helped bring this work to fruition at Westminster John Knox Press. I am especially indebted to Alexa Smith, who initiated the publication process, to Stephanie Egnotovich, who encouraged me patiently through many delays and took a sensitive scalpel to my verbiage, and to Nancy Roseberry for hours of copyediting and finalizing the manuscript.

Introduction

When I began to write this book, I had to ask myself, Why another book on Christian spirituality? The response that surfaced within me had as much to do with purpose and style as specific content. I believe people today are seeking more than well-presented information on the spiritual life. They seek ways to explore and enter into a deeper expression of faith.

The vision for this book is thus primarily experiential and interactive. Each chapter mixes theological and spiritual perspectives with practical suggestions and exercises. You, the reader, are invited to interact creatively with the content.

I harbor no illusions about being an expert on Christian spirituality. I would be inclined to suspect anyone who claimed to be one. There is plenty of room for self-deception in this arena, and no single interpretation of the spiritual life can be considered definitive. The Spirit of God is always free to increase our understanding.

In the pages that follow, I offer my own understanding of what Christian spirituality is and how it may be nurtured among active people in contemporary life. Theological assumptions and definitions are laid out in the first chapter. These are based on my reading of scripture, which remains, I am convinced, our most fundamental and precious wellspring of guidance concerning any spirituality that would call itself Christian. My knowledge of scripture is informed by biblical scholarship but rooted in personal prayer, corporate worship, and those theological interpretations held in common among the great streams of historical Christianity.[1]

I was raised and educated in the Reformed theological tradition, which has taught me, among other things, the value of being ecumenical. Within the broader streams of Christian tradition I have found much that is illuminating and life-giving. I suspect that in times like ours, part of the *new* work of the Spirit among us is the labor of reclaiming timeless truths from the rich heritage of our historic tradition.

I naturally hope that this book will speak to the yearnings and convictions of others within the Reformed tradition, but my primary intent is to make a contribution to the wider conversation of the church on the topic of Christian spirituality. I wish to do so in a way that is accessible to intelligent seekers of many backgrounds.

Who This Book Is For

I imagine those of you who will benefit most from this book are aware of a hunger for greater depth and vitality in your faith life. You know there must be more to a life indwelt by the divine Spirit than what you have experienced, but you are not sure how to gain access to this deeper dimension of life. You realize that there are practices within the spiritual tradition that might lead you deeper—prayer, fasting, discernment—yet you remain mystified about how to approach them, or perhaps anxious at the possibility of being led astray by spiritual frauds. You may feel inexperienced in matters of the spiritual life yet are discriminating enough to know when the "food" you are fed sours on ingestion.

My primary intention is to speak to the spiritual needs and concerns of the ordinary person in the pew. Yet I know from experience that many pastors, church educators, and seminarians are as hungry for guidance in the spiritual life as laypersons, since training for church leadership in most Protestant institutions has not typically included a full range of practices for nurturing inward faith as well as its outward expressions.

This is a book for beginners, yet the term "beginner" is deceptive and paradoxical. The more we comprehend of the spiritual life and the longer we try faithfully to live it out, the more we grasp how simple and primary its essential patterns are. There is a childlike simplicity to Christian spirituality. In a certain sense we never get past practicing the basics. This makes beginners of us all, a truth that is both humbling and freeing. The great sixteenth-century Carmelite nun Teresa of Avila captured the reality well when she wrote, "No soul on this road is such a giant that it does not often need to become a child at the breast again. . . . For there is no state of prayer, however sublime, in which it is not necessary often to go back to the beginning."[2]

Purpose and Scope

My purpose is to help people of faith understand and begin to practice some of the basic disciplines of the Christian spiritual life. Disciplines are simply practices that train us in faithfulness. I have chosen disciplines from the ecumenical tradition that have weathered the test of time, proving to be means of grace to Christians of different histories and cultures. Such practices have consistently been experienced as vehicles of God's presence, guidance, and call in the lives of faithful seekers.

In each chapter I treat one practice, offering (1) sufficient information to understand its nature, including appropriate historical, theological, and biblical references, and (2) questions and exercises of a practical nature to lead into an experiential encounter with the discipline. The exercises suggested within each chapter are oriented to the individual reader but can be adapted for group use. Group questions and exercises are offered in Appendix A, which could function as a leader's guide.

Because my intent is practical and experiential, this book could be said to be more *formative* in its approach to the spiritual life than *informative*. More precisely, the information in the book is offered in the service of faith formation. My aim is to engage mind and heart together in seeking nourishment for our spiritual hunger.

No introductory book on the spiritual life can be comprehensive. I am keenly aware of the compromises made in treating certain topics and omitting others. For example, I could have included a chapter on journal keeping, which is considered by many to be "a discipline for our day." I chose, instead, to weave journal-keeping suggestions into each chapter as it seemed appropriate. Within the limited scope of this book, the selection of topics inevitably represents my own sense of the "weight" of these practices relative to other possibilities.

I have tried to arrange the chapters with a meaningful flow between topics. In chapter 1, I discuss the widespread spiritual hunger of our time, suggesting where we might look for satisfaction. I introduce basic terms and perspectives concerning the Christian spiritual life. In chapter 2, I consider the practice of spiritual reading, understood primarily as meditative reading of scripture. For Protestants generally (but not exclusively), hearing and responding to God's Word alone or in a small group is a priority in the spiritual life.

The nature and practice of prayer is treated in chapter 3. The spiritual life receives its very heart and soul in prayer, a practice that for Christians is embedded in meditation on scripture. In chapter 4, I take up the role of public worship in our spiritual formation. This discussion is placed after that of spiritual reading and prayer only because personal reading and prayer immeasurably enrich our experience of corporate worship. Worship remains the foundation and context for every spiritual practice, especially those of a personal or "private" nature.

Fasting is closely associated with both public worship and private prayer in Christian tradition. In chapter 5, I look at fasting in the larger context of abstaining from excessive attachments and nurturing simplicity of life. Fasting and penitence are closely associated in most religious traditions, including Jewish and Christian tradition. Chapter 6 encourages us to reconsider the ancient art of self-examination and confession.

Christians historically have not understood confession to be solely a private matter between God and the individual. To examine one's heart alone can lead to despair, self-deception, or unhealthy scrupulousness. Chapter 7 is an introduction to the importance of consulting with another Christian who can act as a guide or mentor in spiritual growth.

In chapter 8, I consider the central Christian practice of hospitality. Here I move beyond disciplines that focus primarily on our relationship with God, even when they involve us with and affect others. Hospitality directly and visibly expresses our spiritual kinship with every human being and with the whole creation. It is both a *means* of God's transforming grace for us and a fruitful *expression* of the Spirit working in us for the sake of others.

In chapter 9, I consider what it might mean to devise a "rule of life" for ourselves from what we have learned by working through the preceding chapters. The connection between personal and corporate disciplines should be very clear at this point, not as a logical argument but as an experienced reality.

Appendix A is a collection of questions and exercises designed to make the book useful as a resource for small groups or classes. An annotated bibliography, based on categories related to chapter headings, emphasizes books that are accessible in language and practice.

How to Use This Book

This book is meant to be *used*, not simply read. It is intended to be a catalyst for your own thinking, imagining, feeling, intuiting, willing, and experiencing in relation to your faith. The margins serve three purposes.

First, they feature quotations from writers representing a wide spectrum of Christian traditions, to help illuminate the basic text. (Source information for these quotes and for chapter epigraphs is included in Appendix B.) Second, they contain questions to contemplate and suggestions for written reflection to help you assimilate the chapter content in relation to your personal experience. Third, they provide space to jot down ideas arising from your reading.

You may use this book in several ways. One is to separate reading and reflection into two distinct activities. You may choose to read a chapter through once without regard to marginal materials and then read over it again, stopping to reflect on quotes, questions, and other exercises as you feel drawn to them.

Another way is to treat the book as "spiritual reading," as described in chapter 2. In this case, you would read at a moderate pace and pause frequently to think and absorb as you read. The marginal materials would be taken in as you go, giving both permission and structure to your reflective interaction with the text. The book is written and formatted to be read in this second way, but if the first method better suits your way of learning you should certainly use it.

This book covers a great deal of ground on the subject of spiritual practices. You should not expect to launch into everything at once, even if you feel inspired to do so. Similarly, there is no need to be discouraged at the thought of all the things you *don't* do. My purpose is to introduce you to a variety of possibilities for enriching your spiritual life. Pay attention to what you feel especially drawn to, and why. God would much rather that we learn to be faithful in a few humble commitments than that we continually despair over our failures because we take on too much.

A good way to read this book is with a small community of other seekers. If you study, pray, and practice with just one chapter between gatherings, you will not run the risk of getting spiritual indigestion by trying to take it all in at once. The group process suggestions in Appendix A will help guide your class or community through each chapter.

I hope this book will add a unique voice to the lively conversation going on in our church and culture—a dialogue concerning how we nurture and sustain spiritual vitality in contemporary life. I trust that reading and reflecting on what follows will do more than edify—that it will draw you into a courageous and joyful exercise of those practices that may yield an experiential knowledge of God. God's own challenging guidance and providential grace is more than sufficient to satisfy the hunger in each of our lives and communities of faith. When we begin to take spiritual practices seriously, the possibilities for personal and corporate transformation are truly beyond our imagining! May grace attend your reading and reflection.

Notes

1. The three main streams are Eastern Orthodox, Roman Catholic, and Protestant. The theology they hold in common is expressed most concisely in the ecumenical creeds, particularly the Apostles' Creed and the Nicene Creed, which were adopted by the church before any major schism occurred.
2. *The Life of Teresa of Jesus: The Autobiography of St. Teresa of Avila*, trans. and ed. E. Allison Peers (Garden City, N.Y.: Image Books, 1960), 145.

1   Hunger and Thirst for the Spirit
The Spiritual Yearning of Our Time

O God, you are my God, I seek you,
  my soul thirsts for you;
my flesh faints for you,
  as in a dry and weary land
    where there is no water.

Psalm 63:1

Signs and Seasons

There is a hunger abroad in our time, haunting lives and hearts. Like an empty stomach aching beneath the sleek coat of a seemingly well-fed creature, it reveals that something is missing from the diet of our rational, secular, and affluent culture. Both within and beyond traditional faith communities, a hunger for spiritual depth and integrity is gaining momentum.

For some of us, the hunger is amorphous. Like free-floating anxiety, it lurks just below the surface of consciousness. Perhaps we feel an emptiness that leaves us restless for a larger meaning and purpose in life. Perhaps we sense that we are sailing through life in a rudderless ship. Something is missing. Something is out of balance. But it remains nameless.

For others of us, the hunger is recognizably spiritual. We know there is a vacuum inside us that will suck up an infinite supply of thrills, goods, and successes without satisfying the human heart. We are aware of needing a transcendent compass. Suffering has opened us to questions for which there are no easy answers—perhaps no answers at all. We have come to believe that only a power beyond this life can give meaning to our choices and circumstances.

Yet older patterns of religious life may seem antiquated and inadequate. For the first time, people are separating their spirituality from religion. "Institutional religion" has become a negative phrase. In line with our cultural individualism, people find it natural to devise private belief systems that are independent of historical faith communities or traditions. Many seekers consider themselves "spiritual" but not "religious."

The spiritual thirst of our time has become a social phenomenon. People from all walks of life and many faiths are searching with renewed intensity for a spiritual center. Some drink from the wells of Asian religions, Native American traditions, or New Age theories and practices. Within more traditional Christian communities, many speak of being on a "spiritual journey." Church basements are filling up with Twelve-Step "recovery spiritualities." Retreat centers are bursting at the seams. Some Roman Catholic religious houses have become retreat facilities for an influx of Protestants seeking knowledge of prayer, contemplative life, and spiritual direction. Psychotherapists report more clients asking questions of a spiritual nature. Seminarians clamor for courses that will address their spiritual questions in more than a purely academic way.

A sea change is occurring within and beyond our churches. Its current expressions have been building for at least a generation. In terms of its pervasive character in American society, I suspect what we are witnessing today may be close to the significance of the Great Awakening in the eighteenth century. The change represents a powerful impulse toward spiritual wholeness at a time of unprecedented personal and social fragmentation. The spiritual yearning is evident well beyond the boundaries of traditional faith communities.

Rhymes and Reasons

History shows that movements of religious renewal wax and wane. Why should a tide of spiritual ferment be rising in our time with such force? Many factors contribute to the current phenomenon. Some are cultural, some are personal, and some I believe can only be described as spiritual.

Cultural Factors

Four cultural factors are readily discernible. First, from the time of the Enlightenment, Western culture has been increasingly steeped in the worldview of rationalism. Rationalism makes reason the highest authority in determining what is true. Its expression in the modern scientific mind has little sympathy for anything that cannot be measured, quantified, and categorized. Invisible realities that do not yield to scientific inquiry are generally dismissed from the realm of possibility. Consequently, we have suffered from the loss of a sense of sacredness in life. God is simply not "in the picture" in the cultural assumptions of scientific rationalism. This reduction of life to narrow and mechanistic categories of reality is no longer adequate for many people.

Second, technological advances have led to exponential change at virtually every level of our lives. The rate of change over the past century has resulted in enormous social dislocation and stress. Many people long for some center of stability amid such rapid and pervasive change.

Third, we live in a culture that glorifies superficial values. As a society we have little deep sense of purpose that calls us to sacrifice individual desires for the sake of a larger good. I recently spoke with a young couple who are raising three children. They are painfully aware that our cultural values make it a rigorous challenge to live out authentic faith. They want to be able to swim against the tide of Madison Avenue hype that seems to be sweeping their children away in a flood of unimaginative toys, name-brand clothes, and sports idols. They are typical of many who are searching for values that nourish human growth in a responsible community. They can see that material wealth, sexual attractiveness, physical prowess, and social status are the spiritual equivalent of empty calories. We are beginning to starve for values of enduring substance.

Finally, our culture is increasingly paralyzed by fear. Fear of violent crime, drugs, and guns currently dominates our political and social landscape. Fear of losing jobs and health insurance looms large for many Americans. The threat of nuclear and ecological disaster is still present. We harbor deep pessimism about the ability of human beings to create just and secure orders of life. These fears contribute to both a pervasive anxiety and a desire for secure faith.

Personal Factors

At the personal level, three factors bear especially on our spiritual hunger. First, suffering and tragedy seem to be powerful catalysts for moving people toward spiritual perspectives on life. Our rapidly changing society has brought new forms of human suffering. Painful experiences cry out for explanation. Every spiritual tradition has its theodicy, a framework for interpreting human suffering. We want to know how God is related to our pain. Suffering makes us aware of our need for a larger framework of meaning and purpose in life.

Second, many people are restless and dissatisfied with the church as they have experienced it. God has not come alive for them through traditional religious institutions. I know a man who has dutifully attended worship and served as a church trustee for years. He is still mystified by the language of faith. Words about God seem mere words—beautiful and hopeful, but unconnected to the world he knows. This man would like to believe, but he does not experience the reality of God in his life. The faith of his friends both encourages him and makes him feel even emptier. Deep inside he yearns for his faith to catch fire. Like this man, many who feel dissatisfaction in their faith experience continue seeking spiritual truth through the church. Others have chosen to look elsewhere. All of them know a deep hunger for direct experience of God rather than "second-hand faith."

The longing for direct, firsthand experience is the source of the tremendous interest on the part of Protestants in the mainstream denominations in the subject of spirituality.

Howard L. Rice

Third, people who *have* had vivid experiences of God in their lives often find no place to share them in traditional churches. A woman I know had a profound experience when she was fourteen. In a time of solitude, she heard a very clear voice that seemed startlingly more real than any human voice. The voice said, "You are my beloved child; walk with me, and you will heal my people." She felt flooded with a sense of well-being and peace and was powerfully moved to serve God. Yet until we met, she had never felt free to share her experience with anyone in her family or church. She learned early on that people who "hear voices" are considered mental cases. This woman did not know there was a framework from her faith tradition to help her interpret what had happened. She often doubted whether her experience was real because she could not imagine anyone accepting it as real. Unless a priest, pastor, or parishioner is willing to hear and take such experiences seriously, people like this woman are left with no guidance for integrating their own experience into their faith or church life.[1]

4

Spiritual Factors

Beneath these specific cultural and personal factors lies a deeper reason for the spiritual hunger of our day. Human beings are innately religious. We harbor a bedrock desire for a transcendent wellspring of meaning and purpose in life. While sociologists may attribute the universal human religious impulse to psycho-social need, people of faith believe that we are *made* for relationship with God. Therefore until that relationship is sought and found, there will always be an existential emptiness at the core of our being. Centuries ago Saint Augustine confessed to God, "You have made us for yourself, and our heart is restless until it rests in you."[2]

God is the primary factor behind the spiritual seeking of our time. It would appear that the Holy Spirit stirs things up when our societies and sacred institutions get complacent or corrupt. God's intentions are surely the most crucial force behind the swelling tide of spiritual hunger today. Without the fidelity of divine purpose, all we can hope for when the wave of hunger has crested is the frothy aftermath of a fad. But with the integrity of divine purpose, we can trust that a truer and more authentic spirituality may emerge from our restless search for soul sustenance.

You called, you cried, you shattered my deafness. You sparkled, you blazed, you drove away my blindness. You shed your fragrance, and I drew in my breath, and I pant for you. I tasted and now I hunger and thirst. You touched me, and now I burn with longing for your peace.

Saint Augustine

Approaching the Table

Before we turn to the food and drink that might satisfy our hunger and quench our thirst, I need to clarify the key terms I use in this book and name my basic definitions and assumptions.

What Is Spirituality?

The term *spirituality* has gained wide currency in our cultural imagination, including our churches. Protestants are attracted to the word in part because they perceive it as fresh and open to meaning. Older terms like "piety" or "devotion" have become weighed down with negative associations.

5

Piety, a word once endowed with respect, now suggests to many a saccharin sentimentality or the delicate, easily shocked conscience of moral rigidity. Our caricature of a pious Christian has eyes rolled heavenward and hands permanently joined at the fingertips. Indeed, many would rather be taken for secular humanists than pious Christians!

The word *devotion* has suffered a similar though less damaging fate. It retains the sense of inward reflection that attracts many to the word *spiritual*. It also signifies a heart given over in love and adoration to the beloved. Yet the notion of complete devotion to anyone or anything may suggest excessive emotional attachment or lack of objectivity. The term also has the ring of a potentially superficial and external exercise: "I do my five-minute devotions every morning."

In some instances, I support restoring the positive meaning of older terms. It seems clear, however, that *spirituality* has become the contemporary word of choice for expressing how we live with God in this world. As it is now a reasonably permanent fixture in our religious vocabulary, we had best be clear what we mean when we use the term.

I prefer to begin with a more biblical phrase, "the spiritual life." Scripturally speaking, the spiritual life is simply the increasing vitality and sway of God's Spirit in us. It is a magnificent choreography of the Holy Spirit in the human spirit, moving us toward communion with both Creator and creation. The spiritual life is thus grounded in relationship. It has to do with God's way of relating to us, and our way of responding to God.

In Christian experience, the work of the Holy Spirit is to conform us to the image of Christ:

> Now the Lord is the Spirit, and where the Spirit of the Lord is, there is freedom. And all of us, with unveiled faces, seeing the glory of the Lord as though reflected in a mirror, are being transformed into the same image from one degree of glory to another; for this comes from the Lord, the Spirit. (2 Cor. 3:17–18)

The human creature was made in the image and likeness of God (Gen. 1:26–27), yet we obscured and distorted that likeness in the Fall. Christ is "the image of the invisible God" (Col. 1:15) in all its original purity. When we are "clothed with Christ," the truth of our humanity is restored to us and the image of our Creator

What does spirituality mean to you? Write out your own definition here.

6

begins to emerge with clarity. In Christ we are reshaped according to the pattern we were created to bear.

This reshaping is the basic meaning of *spiritual formation* in the Christian tradition. The term *formation* lies at the heart of words like conformation, reformation, and transformation. It invites us to consider: What or whose form are we seeking? What, in our personal or corporate life, needs to be re-formed?

The apostle Paul clearly believed that Christ could be formed in his followers: "My little children, for whom I am again in the pain of childbirth until Christ is formed in you" (Gal. 4:19). He urges, "Do not be conformed to this world, but be transformed by the renewing of your minds" (Rom. 12:2). What he means by the renewal of our minds finds expression in Philippians 2:5: "Let the same mind be in you that was in Christ Jesus." Christ is formed in us not just personally but corporately. The mind of Christ is to shape and direct the entire body of Christ. Here we receive our truest identity, meaning, and purpose. Drawing on Paul's theology, we can say that "spiritual formation" is conformation to the image of Christ by the indwelling of the Holy Spirit.

If the Christian spiritual life has to do with Christ being "formed in us," what is spirituality? In one sense spirituality is simply the *capacity* for a spiritual life—the universal human capacity to receive, reflect, and respond to the Spirit of God. But in a more practical sense, spirituality is the *way we realize* this spiritual potential. It involves conscious awareness of, and assent to, the work of the Spirit in us. Spirituality points to a path—to choices of belief, value commitments, patterns of life, and practices of faith that allow Christ to be formed in us.

The Character of the Spiritual Life

The spirituality I am describing is dynamic. God's Spirit is continually challenging, changing, and maturing us. Although we may be able to point to a single and decisive conversion experience, remaining faithful involves a journey of continual conversion. It can never be said in our lifetime that we have "arrived." The spiritual life invites a process of transformation in the life of a believer. It is a process of growing in gratitude, trust, obedience, humility, compassion, service, and joy. As we

What do you think it means for us to be made in God's image and likeness? How do you understand "the image of Christ"?

What does the word formation *mean to you? What does "conformed to the image of Christ" suggest? Does it sound attractive or make you nervous? Why?*

Good - Because I have an image of Christ which draws me to him and gives me peace.

7

deepen our relationship with God, we begin to choose God's ways and purposes as our own.

It should be clear that Christian spirituality begins with God, depends on God, and ends in God. We owe our capacity to be spiritual to the grace of One who creates us free to share love with our living Source. The old mystics were fond of saying that we are *capax Dei*, that is, capable of receiving and embodying divine life. Paul's prayer in Ephesians 3 ends with the remarkable words, "so that you may be filled with all the fullness of God"! We are linked to the Spirit in a way we cannot adequately conceive or describe, but can experience and express in our life.

Christian spirituality is thus initiated and sustained by One who lives both within and beyond us. This means that while God chooses to be known to us in and through personal experience, the divine Being always transcends personal experience. God is mercifully free from the distortions that personal experience is inevitably subject to. For example, we cannot force God to conform to our agenda for the world; we cannot manipulate God with our prayers; and we cannot achieve spiritual growth through sheer grit and will power. The spiritual life is not a task of self-reformation. There is no fix-it-yourself kit, no manual promising "five easy steps to the complete spiritual person."

Spiritual growth is essentially a work of divine grace with which we are called to cooperate. Free and active cooperation is our share of the labor. But experience teaches that we don't cooperate with God's intentions for us easily. Opening ourselves to the work of the Spirit requires effort and discipline.

This raises a natural question about the relationship between divine grace and human free will. Is it God's work or our work that makes things happen? The answer, of course, is yes! The marvelous paradox of our relationship with God is that grace undergirds rather than undermines our free choice. So Paul can urge his flock to "work out your own salvation with fear and trembling; for it is God who is at work in you, enabling you both to will and to work for his good pleasure" (Phil. 2:12).

A metaphor from early Christian tradition may help us grasp more clearly the nature of this relationship. Observe a sailboat. It cannot move by its own power but must rely on the force of wind, over which neither sailboat nor sailor has control. Still, a sailor can shift the position of the boat by adjusting tiller and sheets so that the sails catch the wind. Free will is like the sailor.

Reflect on John 21: The disciples fished all night and caught nothing. Jesus told them to cast their nets again. Does this story suggest anything to you about the relationship between human labor and divine grace?

God's divine grace produces! we "produce" nothing on our own.

Though it is sometimes a struggle, we can choose to hold the boat of our life steady into the wind of the Spirit. Then our efforts are supported and directed by grace. One caution: Once we have opened our sails to that wind, we need to be prepared to go where the Spirit blows!

The sailboat metaphor will get leaky if we push it too far. In the end, even our ability to hold our boat steady into the wind rests on God's grace. All is grace, yet all depends on our willingness to work freely with grace. The magnificent truth of Christian faith is that the work of divine grace makes our efforts not less our own, but more.

The Role of Spiritual Disciplines

Certain practices can help us attend to the work of grace in our lives and our times. These practices—such as scriptural meditation, prayer, and discernment—are often called spiritual disciplines. What is the nature of discipline and its place in spiritual growth?

"Discipline" often seems a harsh word. It can conjure up images of parents punishing disobedient children or of strict teachers prowling classrooms with rulers in hand. Yet we also appreciate the value of discipline. We admire musicians, athletes, and scholars who develop their full potential through rigorous study and practice. Some of us would be happy to maintain a well-organized desk! How often I hear others echo my own struggle: our hopes for regular spiritual practice are eroded by time constraints, fatigue, or simple inertia and procrastination. Discipline does not come naturally to most of us; it must be cultivated.

I have just used the term *discipline* in two distinct ways. The first carries the sense of order imposed by an authority on someone subject to that authority. The second signifies a training regimen freely taken on for long-term personal benefit. The purpose of the second is generally mastery of a field or personal growth. Both kinds of discipline involve a "rule" or pattern of behaviors, but what motivates each is clearly different.

Spiritual disciplines are practices that help us consciously to develop the spiritual dimension of our lives. Like an artist who wishes to develop painting skills, or an athlete who desires a strong and flexible body for the game, a person of faith freely chooses to adopt certain life patterns, habits, and commitments in order to grow spiritually. There is nothing externally imposed about spiritual disciplines. In adopting them, we simply recognize that our innate spiritual aptitude cannot develop fully without practice.

We will choose spiritual disciplines only if we have a strong desire to grow. If our desire to develop spiritually is not deep enough to overcome our resistances, we will find ourselves unable to maintain any discipline, however good our intentions. If this is our current state, there is no reason to berate ourselves. Desire cannot be forced or manufactured; it can only be discovered in freedom. Yet even a little desire can be encouraged to grow stronger through the practice of discipline, like a spark fanned into full flame or a seedling cultivated into full growth.

It may help to understand that spiritual disciplines are not ends in themselves. Rather, they are simply means of grace. As the Quaker pastor and writer Richard Foster puts it, "By themselves the Spiritual Disciplines can do nothing; they can only get us to the place where something can be done.... [They are] the means by which we place ourselves where [God] can bless us."[3]

Spend some time reflecting on the garden as a metaphor for the human heart. You might want to read the parable of the sower (Mark 4:1–20).

Spiritual disciplines are like garden tools. The best spade and hoe in the world cannot guarantee a good crop. They only make it more likely that growth will be unobstructed. The mystery of maturation lies in the heart of the seed, and the outcome of planting depends largely on the vagaries of weather. Still, tools are important in helping to ensure that planted seeds will bear fruit. Tools can remove stones and roots, aerate the soil, weed and water the garden.

Disciplines like prayer, scriptural reflection, and hospitality have the character of garden tools. They help keep the soil of our love clear of obstruction. They keep us open to the mysterious work of grace in our heart and our world. They enable us not only to receive but to respond to God's love, which in turn yields the fruits of the Spirit in our lives.

Every spiritual discipline tutors us in relationship. Words like *disciple* and *discipline* share the root meaning of being taught. Jesus' disciples were taught by his words and example in a living relationship. Our discipleship is no different. It grows in the embrace of a living relationship with the divine Spirit. What a remarkable promise it is (John 16:13) that the Spirit of Jesus will be a present teacher to those who follow him with their whole heart!

10

I have heard spiritual disciplines described as "windows onto grace." This lovely phrase serves also to warn us against the possible misuse of spiritual practices. As long as a discipline is like a window—transparent to God—it is a genuine means of grace. But a discipline can become opaque, reflecting only our distorted motives. For example, we might seek nothing more than a peaceful or ecstatic experience in our practice of contemplative prayer, or hospitality might simply be a means of self-display if our aim is to impress people with it. Spiritual disciplines, like all good things, can be pursued for the wrong reasons. If our motives are distorted, the practice will not yield good results.

We need to remember, of course, that our motives are almost always mixed to some extent. If we were to wait until they were completely pure before practicing a spiritual discipline, we would never get started! Better to begin practicing and pray that over time we will be given grace to live into greater purity of heart. As our own desires and intentions become aligned with God's intentions for us, we find ourselves free to follow and serve Christ. Discipline makes us disciples with a clear and joyful purpose.

It would be nice if we could simply "practice the presence of God" in all of life, without expending energy on particular exercises. But the capacity to remember and abide in God's presence comes only through steady training. If we wish to see, name, and love Christ "in the flesh" of daily existence, we will eventually need some kind of intentional practice of spiritual discipline.

Food and Drink: Finding Spiritual Nurture

Our spiritual hunger is evidence of the timeless human need for a real and abiding relationship with God. God is the one who calls us into relationship, and God does everything possible to restore us when we have wriggled out of the mutual demands of this relationship. God's love lies at the root of our hunger for God. Love is *God's hunger* for relationship with us. Has it ever occurred to us that God is starved for our companionship?

Not long ago I was stricken by the comments of a colleague, a woman of deep prayer. She was describing what she had heard in response to the question she puts before Jesus each morning. Her question is, What do you want me to tell the people? For

11

many years the response she received was, Tell the people that I love them. Then one day the reply came: Tell the people that I miss them.[4]

Is our God a lover blinded by grief, calling out through the ache of our hunger—calling us to come home and be nourished with real life once again? Can we begin to see our hunger as a response—feeble, fitful, and fearful, but a response nonetheless? It is a response to God's anguished hunger for the creatures fashioned by divine hands for relationship with the divine heart.

We are like the prodigal son of Jesus' parable—children far from home and starving. Have we decided to go home? If so, what path will set us toward the destination of our Creator's heart? Where do we turn to find nourishment for the parched places of our souls? What food and drink will be adequate to our need? We often do not know where to look for resources, how to find others who share our yearning, or how to voice our longings.

This book is an effort to help us find and partake of food and drink for the spirit. The resources we will explore are drawn from our full Christian heritage. None of the practices are new, but many have been lost to our knowledge. Our current spiritual hunger is partly due to being out of touch with traditional practices that could feed us. When we are severed from our roots, we are like plants without nourishment. Yet each practice needs to be interpreted and tested in our own time if it is to be recovered as a valuable source of spiritual nurture.

For example, examination of conscience, fasting, and spiritual guidance are relatively unknown within most contemporary Christian communities. They are "lost arts" well worth recovering. Disciplines of worship, scriptural reflection, and prayer are still practiced as abiding resources of faith, but even these may not be experienced in helpful ways. Worship can feel flat and artificial; scripture may seem impenetrable and archaic; prayer can feel like rote repetition or an exercise in frustration. Fortunately, there are perspectives and practices from the larger tradition that can help us experience well-worn disciplines in fresh and life-giving ways.

If we are to fruitfully reappropriate classic disciplines for the Christian life, we need to be willing to engage "tradition" creatively. We also need to be alert to our current context so we can

me?

Do these questions fit your experience? If not, how have your experiences been different? What frustrations have you felt in seeking answers?

discern where the winds of the Spirit are blowing now. Human beings make sense out of life by continually threading old and new together.

Tradition

Do you have ambivalent feelings about the word *tradition*? Sometimes we gaze wistfully on older traditions that seem to offer stability in a confusing world. Yet our cultural impulse is to discard the old for bright new possibilities and paradigms that would be thwarted by tradition. Many in the church today view Christian tradition as impeding creative change. But the irony is that the truest aspects of Christian tradition are the most radically creative and life-changing. Indeed, tradition itself provides us with criteria for "sorting living truths from dying customs."[5]

Just what is tradition? Scripture itself is an expression of ancient Jewish and early Christian tradition. Christian tradition came to include central creeds and confessions by which the church interpreted basic elements of the gospel theologically. The writings of great theologians, mystics, and reformers from the early church to the present figure into tradition. For some branches of Christianity, tradition also includes liturgical practices and oral legacies.

Tradition tracks a living faith through its history, helping us find markers that let us follow the path today. Some of those markers allow us to enter into the peculiar world of scripture so that it again becomes a vital Word for us. Some markers reveal the rich ore of contemplative prayer and meditation available for us to mine. Voices from the tradition create a kind of symphony from which we may catch a melody that moves us to sing our own praises in worship. While not all of tradition is worth preserving, there are so many riches to be recovered from its storehouse that we should be glad to sift the treasures from the sand in which they are buried!

In reappropriating the best of Christian tradition, we discover a feast for hungry hearts. Indeed, I might caution against a temptation to gluttony! The sources are rich and need to be taken in small bites. Each chapter of this book is designed to help us sample the soul feast of our historic heritage.

Do you remember Tevya in Fiddler on the Roof *invoking "tradition" as the reason for opposing any sort of change? What does the word evoke in your own experience?*

A challenge to look at tradition @ open eyes and an unbiased thought and expression.

Glenn Hinson, an eminent church historian, argues that there is a difference between deep tradition and mere convention. Ponder this distinction and write down what you think it means.

Hesitations about Partaking

Whenever we talk about moving closer to God, it is natural to feel certain reservations. Intimacy with the primordial Mover and Shaker of the universe can be a daunting prospect. Even while we feel drawn to our living Source through the hunger divinely implanted in our hearts, we also feel repelled at times. The reasons for this peculiar resistance are various.

We may feel too small and insignificant for God to bother with, or not feel at all sure that God could love us as we really are. Such feelings will make us hesitate to seek God wholeheartedly. We may be afraid of what we would encounter if we came too close to God. It is one thing to be told what God is like; it could be another thing altogether to discover the truth for ourselves! What is God really like? Can we survive contact? Perhaps we feel anxious over what God might demand of us if we got too close. Maybe God would ask us to give up certain relationships, life dreams, or things we enjoy. God might call us to do something we felt we couldn't do, like work with the poor or become a missionary in Borneo. Fears like these can certainly make us hesitant to explore the deeper reaches of relationship with our Creator.

Then there are questions about the legitimacy of spirituality itself. Unhappily, our Christian tradition has fostered an unhealthy split between earth and heaven, body and spirit. Those committed to the social implications of the gospel are concerned that spirituality is an easy escape from active discipleship in the world and might simply be another form of self-fulfillment that finally denies God's purposes for human community. If the spiritual life means navel gazing while Los Angeles burns, they want no part of it.

These concerns are actually easier to address than is emotional resistance to the spiritual life. The best of our faith heritage has never severed the inner from the outer life, nor the individual from the community of faith. It has never assumed that personal experience is the ultimate measure of truth, or that feelings are a finer gauge of fidelity to God than intellect. Most of us have a genuine concern for coherence between the inner and outer life. We search for unity between personal and social holiness. Horrifying breaches of justice in the world kindle in us a fire to connect prayer, compassion, and righteousness.

Reflect on your feelings about coming closer to God. Are you aware of any anxieties? If so, try to name them below.

No anxieties -.
only anticipation.

Let me be clear about the kind of spiritual life we will be exploring in this book. One of my basic assumptions is that the Spirit of God is the depth dimension of all that we know as life. The spiritual life is not one slice of existence but leaven for the whole loaf. It is the broadest, most encompassing dimension of who we are, embracing in its mystery what we call physical, mental, emotional, and volitional aspects of life. Nothing that we do, think, or imagine is without its impact on our spiritual life, and the spiritual life influences every other dimension of our being. Spirituality is naturally holistic.

The Christian spiritual life, modeled in Jesus, is thoroughly incarnate. It represents a complete unity of spiritual and physical life, including deep feeling, enjoyment of the created order, concern for the welfare of the city, and compassion for all people. Our "journey into Christ" is that lifelong process which our tradition has called sanctification—growth in holiness. But holiness is not some ephemeral, antiseptic state separated from our family, work, or life as a public citizen. It is absolutely practical and concrete. Holy people (saints) get into the dirt and sweat of real life, where light and darkness contend with real consequences. This is where God is at work. If the Word I hear Sunday morning or during my private prayer has no bearing on the way I relate to family, friend, and foe, or how I make decisions, spend my resources, and cast my vote, then my faith is fantasy.

The Spirit insists on transforming us at every level: personal, social, economic, and political. God is Lord of our *whole* life. When we think of categories like prayer and service, contemplation and action, and individual and community as opposites, we simply create false and unnecessary divisions. Nurturing the inner life and addressing social realities are both important aspects of the Christian spiritual life. One is not more "spiritual" than the other, but either by itself is less than a full embodiment of the life we are called to in Christ.

The practices I describe in this book can help us bridge the gap. They move us from deeper personal understanding to alternative ways of being in relationship with others. It is deeply damaging to the church and its members to suppose that we can transform the world if we are unwilling to be transformed personally. What hope have we to offer, what new life do we witness to, if our own hearts are not being made new by God? Jesus' own example reveals that the clarity of a single person who is

How do you understand the connections between inward growth and outward expressions of faith? Have you experienced such a connection? Is it necessary?

My thirst @ staff is that just me?

15

transparent to the Spirit has more impact in God's design than the best theological teachings and most ambitious social ministries. What could happen if an entire congregation or community became a faithful doorway into God's living presence?

I believe that life in Christ is a reality already given to us. It is ours to claim if we have the courage to enter it. And it really *is* new. Life in Christ is different from the patterns of the world we know so well. In place of degradation and abuse, it means reverence and respect for all of life. Instead of the politics of power, it embodies humble and joyful service. In place of retribution and revenge, it offers forgiveness and reconciliation. Beyond the forces of disease and death, it holds out healing and life. Instead of fear and anxiety, it offers trust in God. Life in the Spirit means release from idols and freedom from addictions. Christ provides realistic hope for a realistic life. He is the wellspring for our thirst, the bread for every hunger of the human heart. "O, taste and see that the Lord is good!" (Ps. 34:8). Once we have tasted living bread and drunk living water, we will be able to lead others who hunger and thirst to our common vital Source.

As for the personal anxieties or hesitance we may feel, I suggest we bring them with us into the explorations that follow. Some will evaporate as we come to recognize more about God and ourselves. Others may remain. We need to be gentle with our fears. Testing our experience over time, we can learn to trust the great love of One whose grace transforms us in ways that surpass our wildest dreams!

Notes

1. Howard L. Rice, *Reformed Spirituality: An Introduction for Believers* (Louisville, Ky.: Westminster/John Knox Press, 1991), 7.
2. *Saint Augustine: Confessions*, trans. Henry Chadwick (New York: Oxford University Press, 1991), 3.
3. Richard J. Foster, *Celebration of Discipline: The Path to Spiritual Growth* (San Francisco: Harper & Row, 1988), 7.
4. Loretta Ross-Gotta, director of The Sanctuary (Center for Prayer and Spiritual Renewal) in Holton, Kansas.
5. Avery Brooke, *Plain Prayers in a Complicated World* (Boston: Cowley Publications, 1993), 73.

2 Chewing the Bread of the Word
The Nature and Practice of Spiritual Reading

The law of the LORD is perfect, reviving the soul;
the decrees of the LORD are sure, making wise the simple;
More to be desired are they than gold, even much fine gold;
sweeter also than honey, and drippings of the honeycomb.

Psalm 19:7, 10

Imagine for a moment that you have just received a handwritten letter from a dear friend who lives at a great distance and from whom you have not heard in a long while. What would you anticipate about this letter? Where would you like to be when you open it? Perhaps you can imagine settling into your favorite easy chair or finding a quiet and secluded spot outdoors—a place where you can set aside the unfinished tasks of your busy life and enter into the world of your friend's letter. Eagerness for news could tempt you to devour each page as quickly as possible, yet the sheer delight of spending precious time in your friend's company might compel you to slow down, savoring the words, phrases, and images written specifically for you. In them you discover how it is with one who is dear to your heart, what she or he is thinking, experiencing, and questioning. Here are words that bring a sense of your friend's presence vividly into your life.

Now imagine a different scenario. After several intensely busy days, you spy a newspaper on the coffee table and realize that you've not been keeping up with world events. You pick up the paper and begin paging through, letting your eye rove over headlines, news photos, and captions, scanning articles that catch your interest. Perhaps you are even doing this standing up, hoping to grasp as much information as quickly as possible in order to return to those unfinished tasks.

These two examples may help us to recognize that we have different ways of reading, depending on what we expect to receive. In the case of the friend's letter, words are a means of personal relationship. In the case of the newspaper, words are a vehicle of information. We could say that our approach to the letter is basically relational while to the newspaper it is functional.

The practice of "spiritual reading" has much more in common with the first example than the second. What makes our reading spiritual has as much to do with the intention, attitude, and manner we bring to the words as it does with the nature and content of those words. Spiritual reading is reflective and prayerful. It is concerned not with speed or volume but with depth and receptivity. That is because the purpose of spiritual reading is to open ourselves to how God may be speaking to us in and through any particular text.

The manner of spiritual reading is like drinking in the words of a love letter or pondering the meaning of a poem. It is not like skittering over the surface of a popular magazine or plowing through a computer manual. We are seeking not merely information but formation.

Information is basically utilitarian; it is a means to some other end. We glean facts to strengthen our arguments; we garner knowledge to make our conversation convincing; we seek help with problem solving, ideas for programming, evidence for cases, and illustrations for teaching. The same information may be used for a variety of purposes. I call this approach the strip-mining method of reading; we are preoccupied with digging up little gems of wisdom from their larger context to apply to whatever task is at hand.

Formation, on the contrary, is generally understood as an end in itself. It has to do with the dynamics of change in the human heart, change that reshapes us into the kind of beings God intends for us to be. As this occurs, personal behavior, human relationships, and social structures will be affected quite inevitably for the better, but we do not use formative practices in order to achieve such ends.

Paul exhorts his Christian converts in Rome, "Do not be conformed to this world, but be transformed by the renewing of your minds" (Rom. 12:2). In Paul's view, it is having the "mind of Christ" in ourselves that effects this transformation (Phil. 2:5 ff.). The term *formation*, then, suggests being shaped ever more

We do not always realize what a radical suggestion it is for us to read to be formed and transformed rather than to gather information. We are information seekers. We love to cover territory.

Macrina Wiederkehr

Let the same mind be in you that was in Christ Jesus, who, though he was in the form of God, did not regard equality with God as something to be exploited, but emptied himself . . . and became obedient to the point of death.

Phil. 2: 5–7, 8

18

deeply according to the mind of Christ, who reveals and offers to us our full humanity. Spiritual reading has a formative intent. Through it we seek a living, transforming relationship with God-in-Christ.

Spiritual reading is a meditative approach to the written word. It requires unhurried time and an open heart. If the purpose of our reading is to be addressed by God, we will need to practice attentive listening and a willingness to respond to what we hear. Many kinds of literature can be read in this manner (even newspapers, if we are willing to hear what God may be saying to us through current events). But the primary focus of spiritual reading for Christians has always been scripture, with good reason. The purpose for which the scriptures were written—presenting hearers with God's Word—and the purpose of spiritual reading—allowing ourselves to be addressed by God's Word—are completely consonant. They are as suited to each other as a hand and glove.

Hence . . . if we seriously aspire to the pure contemplation of God [we] must come, I say, to the Word, where God is truly and vividly described to us.

John Calvin

The Nature of Scripture

It is no accident that scripture is called God's Word, but the term may raise for us peculiar questions and tensions. We have, on the one hand, a Bible composed of many kinds of literature, written for various purposes and different audiences. Its words are human words, written by human beings limited in many ways by their own histories and cultures. On the other hand, we have a Bible affirmed through many centuries, and by people of vastly different histories and cultures, as authentically the Word of God for the human creation. It is a body of writings claimed to be holy scripture, inspired of God's Spirit, and cherished as a reliable guide for faith and practice.

Scripture has been compared to a lake whose depths have never been fully plumbed.[1] On the surface it looks like any other lake; that is, we see human words like those in other books. But when we jump into the lake and begin to swim downward, we may be unable to find the bottom. It is as if those human words become transparent to some mysterious and infinite depth we can never fully grasp. Perhaps that is why one writer can say, "Sounding in and through the human words of scripture, like the sea within a conch shell, is another reality, vaster than mind or

19

imagination can compass. God has chosen to be bound to the words of scripture; in and through them, the Holy One comes near."[2]

In traditional Christian understanding, scripture is both God's Word and human word. It is part of God's chosen self-revelation, simultaneously familiar and strange. Thomas Merton, the renowned twentieth-century Trappist monk and writer, expressed this disturbing quality of the Bible when he said that in scripture we discover "the strange and paradoxical world of meanings and experiences that are beyond us and yet often extremely and mysteriously relevant to us."[3]

If scripture truly has this character, we can expect to encounter the divine presence in its pages. It is not that the words magically or mechanically contain God's presence, but that as we allow the same Spirit through which the scriptures were written to inform our listening, the presence of God in and beyond those words becomes alive for us once more. Spiritual reading is relational in nature, a truth beautifully conveyed in the words of the twelfth-century Cistercian abbot William of St. Thierry:

> The Scriptures need to be read and understood in the same spirit in which they were written. . . . You will never understand David until by experience you have made the sentiments of the psalms your own. And that applies to all Scripture. There is the same gulf between attentive study and mere reading as there is between friendship and acquaintance with a passing guest.[4]

In a certain sense, when we are engaged in spiritual reading it is not so much we who read the Word as the Word who "reads" us! Hebrews 4:12–13 puts it in powerful if uncomfortable language: "Indeed, the word of God is living and active, sharper than any two-edged sword, piercing until it divides soul from spirit, joints from marrow; it is able to judge the thoughts and intentions of the heart." If we are open, God's Word will penetrate to our very depths, discerning our secret motives and intentions. As the "sword of the Spirit" (Eph. 6:17), God's Word reveals us truthfully to ourselves and lays us open to radical transformation at those points of our unlikeness to Christ. The simultaneous comfort and discomfort of this nakedness before God's discerning eye is well captured in Psalm 139:

> O Lord, you have searched me and known me.
> You know when I sit down and when I rise up;

This reversal of our normal way of thinking is like the "backwards" perspective of Greek and Russian icons. Instead of receding to a vanishing point in the center of the picture, all the lines of perspective move in toward you, the viewer. The reversal of perspective is intentional. It reveals that spiritual reality is beyond what we contemplate, looking upon us through it. We are not so much the viewer as the viewed.

Find a traditional icon that depicts a building, and observe till you can see the lines of perspective moving toward rather than away from you. How does this make you feel? Think about scripture in terms of this new perspective.

20

you discern my thoughts from far away.
You search out my path and my lying down,
and are acquainted with all my ways.
Even before a word is on my tongue,
O LORD, you know it completely.
You hem me in, behind and before,
and lay your hand upon me. . . .
Where can I go from your spirit?
Or where can I flee from your presence?

Perhaps when we meditate with such a psalm we become aware that our task is not so much to master the text of scripture as to be mastered by the Source of that text. The very best historical-critical knowledge cannot give us control over interpreting the Word. Such knowledge can offer helpful parameters and guidelines, but only God's Spirit can fully interpret God's Word. To use a phrase from an old hymn, "God is his own interpreter, and he will make it plain."

We should point out here that there is an appropriate and important place for an "informational" approach to the scriptures. It involves the discipline of studying the histories, cultures, and languages through which the scriptures come to us. Thomas Merton offers a helpful perspective on the relationship between informational and formational approaches to scripture. An adequate grasp of the biblical text, he says, "requires two levels of understanding: first, a preliminary unraveling of the meaning of the texts themselves . . . which is mainly a matter of knowledge acquired by study; then a deeper level, a living insight which grows out of personal involvement and relatedness. . . . Only on this second level is the Bible really grasped."[5] For Merton, the task of acquiring information is simply the "front porch" of spiritual reading.

Understandings and perspectives gained from biblical study may greatly enrich our experience of spiritual reading of scripture, but the two are not to be confused. German theologian Dietrich Bonhoeffer, who called the practice of spiritual reading simply "biblical meditation," was very clear about the "danger of escaping from meditation to biblical scholarship."[6]

How, then, do we go about spiritual reading with scripture? How do we read in a way that allows us to be encountered by the Reality within yet beyond these familiar words? Since spiritual reading is not concerned with achieving quantity, there is no need to cover a given amount of text. Our intention is

For as God alone is a fit witness of himself in his Word, so also the Word will not find acceptance in [human] hearts before it is sealed by the inward testimony of the Spirit.

John Calvin

Read with a vulnerable heart. Expect to be blessed in the reading. Read as one awake, one waiting for the beloved. Read with reverence.
Macrina Wiederkehr

simply to sink into the words and open ourselves to their meaning in our lives. Instead of analyzing or judging the text, we receive it as given and attend to what may be spoken to us through it. The attitude suffusing spiritual reading is that of the boy Samuel: "Speak, Lord, your servant is listening" (1 Sam. 3:10).[7]

The art of spiritual reading as a reflective assimilation of God's Word reaches straight back into the Jewish tradition of meditation:"Happy are those ... [whose] delight is in the law of the LORD, and on his law they meditate day and night" (Ps. 1:1–2). Its practice in the Christian church was refined and given special weight by Saint Benedict in the sixth century. In Benedictine tradition, spiritual reading is referred to by its Latin title, *Lectio Divina*. Both Roman Catholics and Protestants owe much of their understanding and practice of scriptural meditation to Benedict. Yet few Protestants are aware that figures like the great Reformer John Calvin and the Puritan pastor Richard Baxter advocated a method of reflective meditation with scripture that is directly derived from Benedictine practice. Reformed adaptations of *Lectio* were common practice among the Puritans.[8] Given its significant history, it seems natural to return to the Benedictine source for clarification.[9]

Perhaps if we outline the process of *Lectio Divina* as it has been classically understood and practiced for centuries, we will discover something to enliven our own way of reading scripture.

The Dance of *Lectio Divina*

There are four basic phases in the classic practice of spiritual reading, termed in Latin *lectio, meditatio, oratio*, and *contemplatio*. For a basic English equivalent, add the letter *n* to each. The ordering of these four phases represents a general and often natural sequence of progression, not to be understood rigidly. In practice we may experience great fluidity between them, a weaving back and forth as the Spirit moves us. The image of a dance may be helpful in envisioning the movement between phases and the possibilities for changing "steps" as the "music" shifts.[10] Here, in brief, is a description of each movement.

Lectio literally means reading, from which terms like *lection* and *lectionary* are derived. It signifies the kind of reading we have been portraying: reflective, gentle paced, one-bite-at-a-time. It means reading as if you had a love letter in hand. You allow the words that are pregnant and weighty with meaning to sink in and expand and nourish your heart. With scripture, it entails reading each sentence as if for the first time, expecting that God will address you with a direct and personal message. The message may not be comfortable. Sometimes letters from those who love us contain painful words, but they are offered out of love and may be just what we need to hear. The question behind our reading is, God, what are you saying to me just now?

Meditatio naturally translates as meditation. We need, however, to be clear what we mean by the term. Popular culture, both religious and secular, offers a panoply of meditation methods today. Many have their origins in Far Eastern religious traditions, where meditation involves moving beyond concepts and images to the nameless experience of divine reality. The meaning of meditation in historic Jewish and Christian practice differs in that meditation involves an active mind. The type of mental work is quite specific. It is not the critical, analytical, or formulating work of Bible study, which may inform meditation but remains distinct from it. The mind work of meditation moves us to reflection on where we are in the text. Active imagination can sometimes help us find connections between our life stories and the great story of God's redemptive work with us. Meditation engages us at the level of the "heart" in its biblical sense, where memory, experience, thoughts, feelings, hopes, desires, intuitions, and intentions are joined. This is where we are likely to discover what a given passage means in our lives personally or as a community.

In the practice of the early church, "meditation . . . was a simple repetition of the 'word' received from lectio. . . . The 'word' was repeated in the mind, or even on the lips, until it formed the heart."[11] Thus, the word received from *lectio* was to be taken up and carried in *meditatio* through the day's activities. Meditation essentially became a process of assimilating God's Word over time.

Oratio is related to terms like *oration* and *oratory*, which most of us probably associate with spoken words. In an earlier era, they referred specifically to spoken prayer. In the context of *Lectio Divina*, it means the prayer that naturally flows out of our meditation. Here is our first response to what we have heard and

All-seeing One, above me, around me, within me.
Be my seeing as I read these sacred words.
Look down upon me
Look out from within me
Look all around me
See through my eyes
Hear through my ears
Feel through my heart
Touch me where I need to be touched; and when my heart is touched, give me the grace to lay down this Holy Book and ask significant questions:
Why has my heart been touched?
How am I to be changed through this touch?

          Macrina Wiederkehr

The Word of Scripture should never stop sounding in your ears and working in you all day long, just like the words of someone you love. And just as you do not analyze the words of someone you love, but accept them as they are said to you, accept the Word of Scripture and ponder it in your heart, as Mary did. That is all. That is meditation. . . . Do not ask "How shall I pass this on?" but "What does it say to me?" Then ponder this Word long in your heart until it has gone right into you and taken possession of you.

          Dietrich Bonhoeffer

assimilated in the first two phases of spiritual reading. *Oratio* is the direct cry of the heart to God that rises when we have heard ourselves personally addressed through the Word. Perhaps the Word has touched our pain, and we cry out in hurt, anger or frustration; perhaps God has revealed our sin, and we whisper in confession and repentance; perhaps the Word has evoked gratitude, and our words leap up in thanksgiving; perhaps it has sparked our joy, and we sing out adoration and praise! *Oratio* allows a full range of human responses to tumble forth in heart-felt prayer to the One for whom we were made.

Contemplatio, of course, means contemplation. In Christian tradition, this aspect of prayer bears more resemblance to those Eastern forms of meditation whose purpose is to move us beyond thoughts, words, and images to a kind of "emptiness" or purity of "being." Contemplation is essentially rest, play, Sabbath-time in God's presence. When *oratio* has been played out in all its fury, angst, or exuberance, we come to a place of rest in God. Here there are no expectations, no demands, no need to know, no desire but to be in the divine presence, receptive to whatever God desires to do with us. Here we allow ourselves simply to be, welcoming God's own way of being with us in a "Now" that transcends time. Psalm 131 captures the essence of *contemplatio*:

> Enough for me to keep my soul tranquil and quiet
> like a child in its mother's arms,
> as content as a child that has been weaned. (v. 2, JB)

A weaned child is not seeking anything at its mother's breast; it is content to rest quietly, enjoying the simple comfort of the mother's loving presence, an image of complete peace.

Whatever pattern our steps take, and however the choreography shifts in this dance of *Lectio Divina*, our Partner remains the same—ever faithful and responsive, initiating new twists and twirls in the sacred movement of the divine-human relationship. There may be times when the dance feels expansive and delightful like a ballroom waltz; times when it seems a stormy pastiche of passion, pain, and distraction like some existential modern dance; times when it feels like the slow, gentle motion of water ballet; even times when it seems like no movement at all, unless it be the gentlest, imperceptible cradling of love. The dance of *Lectio Divina* may leave our natural energies drained or replenished, but when practiced faithfully it leads to a deeper knowledge of God and ourselves in relation to God in this world.

Another rather more homely image from our tradition may help us grasp the nature of *Lectio Divina* as a whole. We are invited, by this illustration, to observe a cow. First "the cow goes out and eats some good grass (*lectio*), then she sits down under a tree and chews her cud (*meditatio*) until she extracts from her food both milk (*oratio*) and cream (*contemplatio*)."[12] The image of a cow chewing its cud is perfectly suited to the practice of meditation in the Christian tradition. We can all visualize what it looks like: processing and reprocessing food until it is fully digested! This mundane and pastoral image offers good closure on our discussion of the nature of *Lectio Divina*. It is a matter of taking in the bread of God's Word, chewing on it, and digesting it until it brings forth new life and energy that can be shared with others.

Now, if we can marry the image of the cow with that of the dance, we will have a magnificently realistic notion of the Christian spiritual life!

Invitation to Explore

When you sit down to give spiritual reading a try, you will discover that some preliminary but very practical matters need to be attended to: time, place, and text selection. It is probably clear by now that a discipline of this sort takes unhurried time. I suggest a minimum of half an hour, although a full hour is often more satisfying and fruitful. I also commend the counsel of many experienced saints: give God the best time of your day, not the dregs. It is hard to listen when you are tired. Some of us are "morning persons" and some are "night owls." Take this into consideration in choosing the time you give to God in any spiritual practice.

Choose a place that affords you solitude and reasonable quiet it at all possible. Do everything in your power to reduce the potential for distraction: close your door; unplug the telephone or turn on your answering machine; instruct your children, your house mates, your secretary, or whoever may be concerned not to interrupt you except in emergency. Give yourself permission to be unavailable to others for this time, in order to be fully available to God. Some people find soft music or tapes of natural sounds a helpful backdrop to mask traffic noise or unavoidable distractions.

One easy way to select daily scripture passages is to use a lectionary.[13] If you choose this route, select one genre of reading and stick with it: Old Testament, Psalm, Gospel, or Epistle. Using a lectionary obliges you to reflect on a much wider range of texts than you might be inclined to choose on your own—a healthy discipline in and of itself. You could also base your reading on whole books or letters of the Bible, moving through them sequentially in small portions. (This approach has historically been favored in the Reformed churches in order to preserve the full context of each passage.) A third alternative is to select a passage of scripture that fits your mood or your need (not more than five to ten verses).

Begin by reaffirming that the purpose of this reading is to let yourself be addressed by the living God. Settle yourself quietly, remembering to include your body; find a position or posture that will help you to stay relaxed but alert. Be aware of your intention to listen as openly as possible to the words before you. Release your own "agenda" so you will be ready to receive whatever word God desires to offer you.

Remind yourself of God's presence with you, here and now. You may or may not sense this presence, but you can affirm through faith and trust that the Holy One is attending to you. Offer your gratitude, and ask for the guidance and illumination of the Holy Spirit in your reading.

Turn to the passage and begin to read slowly, pausing between phrases and sentences. For some, silent reading allows the mind to wander, so reading aloud or whispering is preferable. Let the words echo and resonate in your mind; allow meanings to sink in, associations to arise, images to surface. If a word or phrase seems especially significant to you, remain with it, turning it over in your mind and heart. When the sense of immediacy fades, move on to another verse. If it remains meaningful for you, stay with it. Here is a word meant for your ears. Be content to listen simply and openly, like a child listening to a story.

Once you have heard a "word" that seems meant for you, start ruminating on it. Why is this a word for you? What is it about your life right now that needs to hear this word? How is God catching your attention? If the passage is a narrative with people, it may help to imagine the setting of the story, and to envision yourself within it. Who can you identify with? Why? Who do you have trouble identifying with, and why? Imagine how the characters interact, how they feel about themselves and each other. How do the dynamics of the story connect with your own life experience? Is there anything you discover about yourself in this process? What does God seem to be saying to you through this word?

Let your prayer emerge from your encounter with this text. How do you find yourself praying for your own needs, given what you have heard? How does this word move you to pray for others? Allow your prayer to flow spontaneously from the heart, expressing as fully as you can what surfaces out of your listening.

Finally, release all your thoughts, feelings, and intentions to God. There is no further need to listen, reflect, imagine, or respond. There is simply an invitation to return to a place of rest near the heart of God where you may be at peace. God sustains you with love every moment of your life. Delight in this gift, take comfort and joy in it!

If this part of the process seems strange or difficult, read Psalm 131. Allow yourself to be the weaned child, resting on the breast of God.

When you emerge from your contemplation, find a word, image, or phrase that carries the core message you have received. Take this with you into your daily activities and relationships. Let your reflection and prayer continue inwardly as new experiences deepen the word you hear in your spiritual reading.

Other Sources for Spiritual Reading

As I mentioned earlier, the process of spiritual reading can be applied to texts other than scripture, especially to devotional literature or good religious poetry. Great spiritual classics may be read in small portions, savored and reflected upon for personal nurture and edification. You might want to try Francis of Assisi, *The Little Flowers*; Thomas à Kempis, *The Imitation of Christ*; Brother Lawrence, *The Practice of the Presence of God*; John Woolman, *Journal*; or Thomas Kelly, *A Testament of Devotion*.

Let's try out the process of *Lectio Divina* with a passage from the seventeenth-century Carmelite Brother Lawrence, just to see how it could apply to writing other than scripture. Read the passage below at a gentle pace, absorbing the impact of the words and their meaning:

> God has infinite treasures to give us. Yet a little tangible devotion, which passes away in a moment, satisfies us. How blind we are, since in this way we tie God's hands, and we stop the abundance of His grace! But when He finds a soul penetrated with

living faith, He pours out grace on it in abundance. God's grace is like a torrent. When it is stopped from taking its ordinary course, it looks for another outlet, and when it finds one, it spreads out with impetuosity and abundance.[14]

For further readings in the spiritual classics:
Desert Fathers/Mothers, Sayings
Augustine of Hippo, Confessions
Symeon the New Theologian, Hymns of Divine Love
Julian of Norwich, The Revelations of Divine Love
Anonymous, The Cloud of Unknowing
Teresa of Avila, The Way of Perfection; The Interior Castle
Blaise Pascal, Thoughts
John Bunyan, Pilgrim's Progress
William Law, Serious Call to a Devout and Holy Life
Friedrich von Hugel, Spiritual Counsel and Letters
Howard Thurman, Disciplines of the Spirit
Dag Hammarskjöld, Markings
Simone Weil, Waiting for God

Now go back into these words with a mind seeking connections to your own life, and a heart open to being addressed by God in your current situation. Pause to reflect wherever you hear something that seems especially significant. Allow questions to surface: God, do you really have infinite treasures to give me? Do you desire to pour these out in my life? Visualize what happens when a torrent of water is blocked from its normal flow. Ask yourself: What blocks do I put in the way of God's grace? Am I satisfied with too little? How do I become "a soul penetrated with living faith"?

Allow prayer to surface spontaneously from the meditations of your heart. It might be prayer for more vibrant, confident faith; prayer that blocks to faith will be healed and dissolved; prayer for those whose trust in God's grace has been depleted. Then take a few moments to rest in confidence that your desires are known and received in the heart of God. Find joy and peace in this assurance. You have just completed a process of spiritual reading.

If you find older writings difficult to grasp or relate to, begin with the works of modern interpreters of the classic spiritual tradition. Among the best known and loved of contemporary writers are Thomas Merton, Evelyn Underhill, C. S. Lewis, Howard Thurman, Henri Nouwen, and Richard Foster.

Religious poetry, like great devotional classics, can be approached in a deeply personal and prayerful way. In addition, we have the marvelous resource of certain fiction writers whose work embodies profound spiritual insight. These are not generally read in the prayerful manner of spiritual reading per se, but can be absorbed as writings with spiritual intent which inspire deep musing.

It is the attitude we bring to spiritual reading that allows God to transform the text from interesting words to words with the power to change our very being. That attitude is an expectation that we will, through the words we read, be encountered by the loving presence and radical challenge of the living God. That attitude is a willingness to be addressed, discerned, and penetrated by the tender but decisive power of the Holy Spirit. That attitude is a desire to respond fully and freely to what is heard, so that God may restore to us the wholeness of our life in Christ—the divine image obscured in our depths, yet even now being called into the light of day to reveal the glory of the children of God!

Some well-loved fiction writers whose work incorporates the spiritual: Shakespeare, Tolstoy, Dostoevsky, C. S. Lewis, George MacDonald, J. R. R. Tolkien, Nikos Kazanzakis, Dorothy L. Sayers, John Erving, Walker Percy, Flannery O'Connor, Graham Greene, Madeleine L'Engle, Frederick Buechner, Susan Howatch, Edward Hays, and Alice Walker

Notes

1. New Testament scholar Robert Mulholland presented this metaphor in a lecture for a session of the Academy for Spiritual Formation in Sedalia, Colorado, June 1991.
2. John S. Mogabgab, unpublished writings.
3. Thomas Merton, *Opening the Bible* (Collegeville, Minn.: Liturgical Press, 1970), 27.
4. *The Golden Epistle: William of St. Thierry,* trans. Theodore Berkeley (Kalamazoo, Mich.: Cistercian Publications, 1980), 51–52.
5. Merton, *Opening the Bible,* 61–62.
6. In his instructions on meditation to young pastors, Bonhoeffer says flatly, "Whatever happens, do not take the text which you are to preach next Sunday. That belongs to sermon preparation." From Dietrich Bonhoeffer, *The Way to Freedom: Letters, Lectures and Notes, 1935–1939.* See the *Collected Works of Dietrich Bonhoeffer,* Vol. II, ed. Edwin H. Robertson, trans. Edwin H. Robertson and John Bowden (London: William Collins Sons & Co., 1966), 57–61.
7. The relational character of spiritual reading is directly connected to our personal knowledge of God. Parker J. Palmer, in *To Know as We Are Known: A Spirituality of Education* (San Francisco: Harper & Row, 1983), argues eloquently for a view of truth that is personal and relational rather than objective and propositional. Knowledge, like truth, he writes, is not abstract but relational. Spiritual reading encourages this kind of knowledge.
8. Drawing on the writings of Richard Baxter, John White, and Lewis Bayly, Howard L. Rice describes the process of devotional reading used by Puritans in *Reformed Spirituality: An Introduction for Believers* (Louisville, Ky.: Westminster/John Knox Press, 1991), chap. 4.
9. I have also drawn on insights into *Lectio* offered by Robert Mulholland, whose book *Shaped by the Word* I commend. Some of Mulholland's ideas are woven into the fabric of this chapter.
10. The image of dance as a metaphor for the divine-human relationship has very ancient roots. The early Cappadocian Fathers used the Greek term *perichoresis* (*peri*, plus *choresis*, from which our word *choreography* derives, essentially meaning "interpenetrated") to describe the mutual co-inherence of the three Persons of the

Trinity. This is the very life human beings are invited to participate in, "in Christ" through the indwelling of the Holy Spirit.

11. Basil Pennington, "Lectio Divina: Receiving the Revelation," in
Living with Apocalypse, ed. Tilden Edwards (San Francisco: Harper
& Row, 1984), 68.

12. Ibid.

13. A lectionary is a systematic order of scripture readings structured
to correspond to the seasons of the church year (Advent,
Christmas, Epiphany, Lent, Easter, Pentecost, Ordinary Time). It
traditionally offers a selection from the Old Testament, the
Psalms, the Gospels, and the Epistles. Lectionaries move through
the major teachings of scripture in a two- or three-year cycle.

14. *The Practice of the Presence of God*, trans. Robert J. Edmonson, ed.
Hal M. Helms (Orleans, Mass.: Paraclete Press, 1985), 82–83.

3 Communication and Communion with God

Approaches to Prayer

All your love, your stretching out, your hope, your thirst, God is creating in you so that [God] may fill you.... God is on the inside of the longing.

Maria Boulding

I have said that the spiritual life has to do with how God relates to us and how we in turn relate to God. Prayer is the essential expression of this relationship. Like the spiritual life itself, prayer is initiated by God. No matter what we think about the origin of our prayers, they are all a response to the hidden workings of the Spirit within.

God's desire for us ignites the spark of our desire for God. God's guiding heart nudges forth our prayers to be led. The apostle Paul assured us that the Spirit "helps us in our weakness" and "intercedes with sighs too deep for words" (Rom. 8:26). Have you considered what an astonishing promise it is that *the Spirit prays in us,* and does so "according to the will of God?" Perhaps our real task in prayer is to attune ourselves to the conversation already going on deep in our hearts. Then we may align our conscious intentions with the desire of God being expressed at our core.

Prayer expresses our relationship with God. It should not surprise us that this relationship parallels in significant ways our relationship with other persons. It cannot be forced, but grows best in the soil of freedom and mutual commitment. The health and vitality of this relationship depend on clarity and frequency of communication. And any form of intimacy requires time spent in each other's presence, time simply to explore and enjoy the gift of companionship.

Prayer involves freely entering a relationship of communication and communion with God, for the sake of knowledge, growth, and mutual enjoyment. I would like to look at each of these aspects of prayer in turn.

Prayer as Communication

Most of us think of prayer as a conversation with God. This is a natural way to understand prayer and a simple way to practice it. Since the God we know in scripture is personal, we are free to speak with God heart to heart as we might with a dear friend. The content of our conversation may cover a wide range of feelings and experiences, but we will generally express certain classic human attitudes before God: praise, adoration, thanksgiving, confession, and supplication. Our prayers are often weighted toward supplication, which includes petitions for our own needs and intercession for others.

Prayer as conversation with God can be deeply fulfilling. However, if it is the only form our prayer takes, we may begin to sense that something is missing. There are two reasons for this. First, prayer is, by nature, more than conversation. To limit its concept to dialogue is to allow some of the most profound expressions of prayer to escape our notice. Second, our "conversation" may, in practice, be less a dialogue than a monologue that borders on talking *at* God. Some of our prayers resemble "a spiritual shopping list, launched heavenward on the wings of pious words."[1] But God is not, as one author wryly notes, our "cosmic bellhop."[2]

Please understand, there is nothing wrong with supplication. Jesus encourages us to ask with open and persistent trust for what we need (Luke 11:5–13). Still, an unbalanced diet of such prayer over time will probably lead more to frustration than fulfillment. We may start to feel that our prayer is a one-way phone conversation in which all we hear is the sound of our own voice. We may wonder whether we have been heard, whether anyone is on the other end of the line, or whether we are even connected!

Communication is a two-way street. Genuine dialogue asks us to listen as well as to speak, to receive in order to respond. It is the listening side of the communication loop that has been given inadequate attention in most Protestant church teachings

I'm gonna pray now; anyone want anything?

Flip Wilson

32

on prayer. One of the key things we must consider, then, is how we listen to God.

In this part of the chapter I will examine the two primary expressions of prayer as communication: listening to God and speaking to God. I will also look at intercession, a particular instance of communication with God that raises its own set of questions. Finally I will invite you to explore several exercises that may help broaden your experience with prayer as communication. Then we can turn our attention to prayer as communion.

The one condition that precedes *every* kind of prayer is being present to God with conscious awareness. God is always present with us, whether or not we can feel this reality. In a very real sense, then, the foundation of all prayer is being present to the presence of God. Quaker writer and teacher Douglas Steere speaks of "being present where we are" and "not too elsewhere."[3] We have all experienced times when we are present in body but unavailable mentally to one another. When we want to communicate well, we try not to be distracted by time limits, inner thoughts, or external circumstances. The same consideration needs to be given to God. Attending to the moment of encounter is crucial. The breathing, quieting, and "centering" so frequently recommended in prayer are simply ways of helping us focus on the One we wish to be with.

When the muse comes to dine, you have to be at home.
Douglas V. Steere

Listening

Listening is the first expression of communication in prayer. We know that listening precedes speaking in the development of childrens' language skills. The same order applies to the development of our prayer life. Something in our spirit is touched by the Divine Spirit before we are drawn to speak.

But how do we listen to God? Clear communication can be very difficult between people, even with the advantage of inflection, expression, and gesture. How much more confusing it is to communicate with One who is invisible, intangible, inaudible, and inscrutable! Yet God desires to be known and has many ways of communicating with us if we are willing to listen.

As I noted in chapter 1, the place to begin is with scripture. God's self-communication is not limited to the pages of the Bible. Yet if we are open to the Spirit, we can expect to hear God speak

A man prayed, and at first he thought that prayer was talking. But he became more and more quiet until in the end he realized that prayer is listening.

Søren Kierkegaard

to us through writings that are intentionally called God's Word. Through many centuries and in many cultures, the church has found this Word continuing to speak with contemporary power.

For some, the most natural way to listen to God is through Creation. Psalm 19 acknowledges that Creation speaks loudly of divine realities:

> The heavens are telling the glory of God; and the firmament proclaims his handiwork. . . . There is no speech, nor are there words; . . . yet their voice goes out through all the earth . . . (vv. 1, 3a, 4a)

Creation has a unique language of proclamation and praise. Each part of the created order speaks eloquently of its Creator, just as consummate artistry reveals the soul of the artist.

All things are shadows of the shining True: Sun, sea, and air . . . Every thing holds a slender guiding clue Back to the mighty oneness . . .
George MacDonald

The Creator also speaks to us through creation. Are not the distress signals of our earth and the collapse of entire ecosystems a message from God? Surely a Word is being spoken to us through the earth about the urgent need for greater simplicity and more responsible stewardship in our lives. Listening to the earth can be a way of listening to God.

We often hear God's voice through one another. Perhaps someone who knows us well speaks just the word we need to hear in a way we can grasp. Perhaps a complete stranger appears at a crucial moment with a word of encouragement, guidance, or warning. Although most of us are unaware of being used as vehicles of grace for others, God surrounds us with personal messengers every day.

The circumstances of our lives are another medium of God's communication with us. God opens some doors and closes others. A troubling relationship may invite us to attend to something we have not fully faced in ourselves. Through the wisdom of our bodies, God tells us to slow down or reorder our priorities. The happy coincidences and frustrating impasses of daily life are laden with messages. Patient listening and the grace of the Spirit are the decoding devices of prayer. It is a good habit to ask, What is God saying to me in this situation? Listening to our lives is part of prayer.

In recent years, dreams have again been recognized as potential vehicles of divine guidance. The Bible is filled with stories in which God speaks to people through dreams, but we tend to assume this is not the case for ordinary believers today. Modern spiritual writers such as Morton Kelsey and John Sanford, building on the insights of depth psychology, have challenged that assumption. They believe the symbols of our inner life are a natural medium for spiritual insight. As the Bible richly attests, God's way of speaking to us is often mediated by symbols and images. Our dreams exist precisely in this medium. Many people of faith have found it immensely worthwhile to listen to their dreams. It takes practice to learn how to decipher the language of dreams, but persistence can yield a wealth of insight that moves us from psychological to spiritual truths.

Many seekers have discovered that journal keeping can be a way of listening to oneself and to God. Christians through the centuries have written spiritual autobiographies, personal diaries, and journals. Some were written to be read. Others were so personal and confidential that they were burned upon the writer's death. Journal keeping takes varied forms today: a prayer journal might record the insights, questions, and feelings that arise from scriptural meditation; it might be used to record and reflect upon dreams; or it might focus on life issues, struggles, and decision-making processes. One interesting technique in contemporary journal keeping is the device of dialogue with key people in our lives, or with different voices inside ourselves. Writing an imaginary dialogue with a biblical character can be helpful (see "Invitations to Explore," below in this chapter).

Journals give us a record of our spiritual questions, struggles, and insights over time. Reviewing them, we may start to recognize larger patterns: the characteristic marks of our journey; where we have grown and where we have gotten stuck; how we discern God's gracious presence and guidance through it all.

There are more subtle and mysterious ways in which we can hear God speak to us. They often come unbidden, amid ordinary activity or in the quiet of contemplation: a deep intuition, an acutely clear conviction, or a simple inner sense of how things are meant to be. You may have heard someone else say, or found yourself saying, things like, "Somehow I just knew this was what I had to do." Or "It suddenly became perfectly clear to me." Or "The words just came into my head."

The Quakers have a phrase for when something inside us says No: "a stop in the mind." It is a warning that we are moving in the wrong direction, and it normally alerts us to a selfish attitude or behavior. But there may be occasions when, in the course of

To dream is to see love and desires transformed into symbols, words. It should not be frightening, then, that God, who is love, speaks to us through our dreams.

Rubem Alves

Some examples of classic spiritual autobiographies are Augustine's Confessions, *Teresa of Avila's* Life, *and George Fox's* Journal. *Modern spiritual autobiographies and personal journals include Thomas Merton's* The Seven Story Mountain, *Dag Hammarskjöld's* Markings, *and Henri Nouwen's* Genesee Diary.

A fine introduction to various modes of spiritual journal keeping is Ann Broyles's book Journaling: A Spirit Journey.

a perfectly altruistic prayer, there suddenly comes "a stop in the mind." Douglas Steere attests to this experience. It is one of God's ways of telling us not to pursue that particular prayer. Perhaps its aim contradicts the divine design; perhaps the time is not ripe; perhaps it is given to someone else to pray for this person or circumstance.

Anyone can receive such an inner "sense of things," but it becomes more likely as we learn to attune ourselves to the gentle stirrings of the Spirit within and around us. It belongs to the learning of prayer to release our own agenda and wait patiently for God's purposes to be disclosed. Solitude and inner silence provide the most promising environment for hearing the "still, small voice."

Perhaps you are starting to think that virtually anyone or anything can be a divine messenger. I suspect God is trying to get our attention through every aspect of our lives. Are we hearing? Of course, hearing clearly requires discernment as well as attentiveness. Not all the messages we hear are of divine origin. In learning to recognize what is characteristic of God and what is not, the role of a larger community seeking to be faithful to the God of scripture becomes vital.

How many ways there are to listen to God! Perhaps we can now begin to see how broad, multifaceted, and life-inclusive prayer really is.

It does not follow that because a thing is the will of God, [God] will necessarily lead you to pray for it.
James Outram Fraser

Nothing in your life is so insignificant, so small, that God cannot be found at its centre.
Mother Frances Dominica

Speaking

The second primary expression of communication in prayer is speaking from the heart with unreserved honesty. This may seem self-evident. We tend to concentrate on our own words in prayer, assuming that here we are in familiar territory. We may not know what God is trying to say to us, but surely we know what we are trying to say to God! Yet the very familiarity of our thoughts and words may obscure the fact that we are not candid in what we communicate.

Many of us have absorbed tacit or explicit taboos about what we are permitted to bring into prayer. We may have learned, for instance, that doubt, anger, hatred, or despair were inappropriate to express to God. Yet we know what happens to human relationships when negative feelings are suppressed. Communication becomes artificial or breaks down; the two parties become emotionally estranged; intimacy becomes impossible. Why should we imagine it is different with God? In prayer, we need to speak whatever truth is in us: pain and grief, fear and disappointment, yearning and desire, questions and doubt, hope and faith, failure and weakness, praise and thanks, despair and sorrow, anger and, yes, even hatred.

If any of these feelings or experiences seem foreign to our prayer, we need only turn to the Psalms for help. Within their verses the whole range of human passions are expressed with magnificent candor. From them we receive permission to voice the best and worst in us; their words help us cry out to God from the depths of our human condition—both its sordidness and its glory.

It takes practice to learn not to censor our prayer. But trying to keep secrets from God is like the three-year-old who covers her eyes and declares, "You can't see me." God sees into our hearts more clearly than we do. Indeed, God is the one who prompts us to look at what we have swept under the rug of our repressions and rationalizations. The Spirit awakens us to what lies hidden within—sometimes gently, sometimes with a jolt, but always so God can work with our conscious consent to free us for growth.

Prayers of Intercession

One way we speak to God from the heart is through intercessory prayer. Intercession is a concrete expression of the social dimension of prayer. It includes our concerns for other persons, communities, nations, the earth, and our fellow creatures.

People frequently feel confused about praying for others. Often our prayers are not answered in the way we desire or expect. We pray for healing and it does not come, pray for peace and conflict increases. We wonder whether God does not will the good we intend by our prayers, or if perhaps we are not praying rightly. We feel guilty that we do not have enough faith, and we feel angry that evil and suffering are allowed to destroy so much peace and happiness. Sometimes prayer seems to us the feeblest and least desirable option, but the only one left under the circumstances: "All I can do for you is pray."

Stop and reflect. Are there strong feelings in your life that you are hesitant to express in prayer? Can you identify why you hold them back?

How do you respond to the Psalms as a whole? What in particular attracts or repels you?

Intercession is the most intensely social act that the human being is capable of. When it is carried on secretly, it is mercifully preserved from, in fact, almost immunized against, the possible corruptions to which all outer deeds of service for others are subject.

Douglas V. Steere

Views of Intercessory Prayer

In sorting out these difficult matters, it may help to identify how you understand the dynamics. What do you think you are doing and what do you think God is doing when you pray for others? Below are eight possible views of the dynamic of intercession, most of which are derived from scripture. Not all these views are mutually exclusive. Each one expresses how people actually perceive the nature and purpose of their prayer:

What experiences with prayer have shaped your understanding of intercession? How do you feel about "unanswered prayer"? What are your unanswered questions about prayer?

1. By our petitions, reasoning, or arguing, we are changing *God's* attitude and intended action in the world. (See Gen. 18:22–26ff.; Exod. 32:11–14.)
2. By engaging in the struggle of prayer, we find *ourselves* changed, marked by our encounter with the living God. (See Gen. 32:24–30.)
3. In prayer we voice our desires, hopes, needs and frustrations, but cannot assume that these influence God. We are completely dependent on God's sovereign will and action in response. (See Job 7:11–20; 13:3, 19:7; 42:1–6.)
4. In prayer we share our positive life-energies with another person who is mystically connected with us and all other living things, and who can therefore be directly influenced. (No direct corollary in scripture, but a common belief in our time.)
5. In prayer we join our hearts in love with the love of Christ, the great Intercessor, through the unity of the Spirit given in Baptism and sustained by the Eucharist. We give our will to the will of Christ and leave the results to him. (See John 15:1–11; 17; Rom. 8:26–27; Heb. 4:14–16.)
6. In prayer we become aware of God's presence with us and of the Holy Spirit already praying in us, so we do not bring specific prayers, but try to attune and entrust ourselves to that presence and inward prayer. (See Psalm 139; Rom. 8:26–27.)

Do some of these views express your understanding of intercession better than others? Which comes closest to what you think happens when we pray? Perhaps you can identify additional views.

7. When we pray, we simply trust completely that God will respond with a good and appropriate gift in God's own time and way. (See Matt. 7:7, 9–11.)
8. When we pray, we are cooperating with God in willing life and goodness for others, yet we remain vulnerable with God to the limits imposed by evil—limits accepted in the freedom that love creates. (See Mark 14:32–36 and parallels.)

Combining Surrender and Trust

As I consider these views, a particular question keeps assert-ing itself: How can I ask in simple trust for a gift to be granted, and at the same time yield up my will to God? Jesus tells us that if we had faith the size of a mustard seed we could command and it would be accomplished. Yet when we have "mustered up" all the faith we have and still do not receive what we desire, we often try another tack. We add "if it be your will" to protect ourselves from the risk of disappointment. Then if our requests go un-answered we can suppose it was not God's will. But what if God's desire *is* to fulfill to our heartfelt prayers, and other factors inter-fere with this intent?

First we need to examine the attitude with which we approach God in prayer. Do we come to God from an ongoing and com-mitted relationship with God, or casually and at our convenience? Are we using God to fill hopes and wishes that have little to do with God's intentions and purposes for us? God will not be manipulated.

If our relationship is sincere, our prayer will basically be one of thanksgiving for grace already received. The context for "prayers of asking" is a heart offered to God in gratitude, eager to fulfill the divine intent. Jesus says, "If you abide in me, and my words abide in you, ask for whatever you wish, and it will be done for you" (John 15:7). What does it mean to "abide in Jesus"? The image is drawn from the metaphor of a vine and its branches. When we abide in the vine of Jesus' life, a single vital sap runs through us. This sap is a love that pours itself out for others. Jesus gives us everything he has and is. To abide in him is to partici-pate in that outpouring of love.

Here is the posture from which we ask that abundant grace be given those we pray for. We can be confident that grace will be given in a way that best expresses God's loving purpose, with which we are united. It may take time for the grace to become manifest, and perseverance is commended (Luke 18:1–8). The delays are due not to lack of goodwill on God's part but to various blocks on the path of grace. Some of these blocks lie within us, some are in those for whom we pray, and others have to do with the larger "powers and principalities of darkness" contending against God. Since "coercion is not an attribute of

God,"[4] the Holy One must clear the path of grace in ways that do not contradict human freedom. God prefers to work through invitation and attraction, but it takes time for all the players in the delicate web of human relationships to let themselves be won over, and some may simply refuse.

Our confidence in the power of prayer is rooted in the promises that God is continually working for good in the midst of ambiguous situations and that God's purposes will prevail in the end. The divine word does not return to God empty (Isa. 55:11). Love is the only power capable of *enduring* all things. It remains immovable after all else has fallen away. Therefore we can ask for eyes to see where God is already at work and a spirit ready to cooperate with God's activity in any given circumstance. The more fully we entrust ourselves to God, the more freely God's loving purpose can be worked out.

Here is a process that might allow your prayers of intercession to blend the simple trust that you will receive grace with offering your will to God:

> Begin with gratitude and praise, offering your whole heart to God.
>
> If your prayer seems good for all involved, ask boldly with as much faith as you have in you. Faith cannot be forced but can be prayed for: "I believe; help my unbelief!" (Mark 9:24)
>
> Wait with trust and attention for a response.
>
> If you receive no indication that you are *not* meant to receive what you ask for (no "stop" in the mind, no closed doors), keep asking. This is not anxious repetition but trusting perseverance.
>
> If you receive a clear answer to your prayer, let your praise and thanksgiving be sincere and whole-hearted. You may perceive that a gracious response is being given in a way you did not expect; be thankful for new insight into God's mysterious providence.
>
> If you see no indications of grace, ask to be shown if there is something in you that could be blocking it: lack of humility or gratitude, lack of trust, a hidden sin, or the need to forgive someone.

If over time (perhaps several weeks or months, depending on the nature of the situation you pray for) there is no positive response, ask God to reveal to you whether another prayer is more in accord with divine intent. If the substance of your prayer is not transformed and there is still no sign of the grace asked for, God's answer may be no.

Accept that no may be the answer to your prayer. Recognize and affirm that God's no always has a larger and better purpose than we can see.

Seek to discover where God's grace *is* manifesting itself in the midst of this situation, even if not in the manner being asked for. Commit yourself to cooperate as fully as you can with God's work as you discern it.

You should, of course, do everything in your God-given power to bring about what you pray for. "Prayer is not a substitute for action; it is an action for which there is no substitute."[5]

*More things are wrought by prayer
Than this world dreams of.*
Alfred Lord Tennyson

Prayer is a participation in willing God's will. While God's ultimate will cannot be thwarted, the strategy God uses to reach that goal may be infinitely variable. The prayers of committed people become part of the cosmic reality God has to work with. God can use them to "tip the balance" and change the shape of distorted realities in our world.[6] It is not stretching the truth to say that God *needs* our prayers. Such is the dignity and purpose we have been given in the divine scheme of things!

Invitations to Explore

Would you like to try some new approaches to prayer? Here is a small sampling of possibilities. Some may be familiar, others are simply waiting to be introduced.

Imaging Intercession

Consider using your imagination rather than words as a primary way of prayer. Here is a simple way to pray using imaging as a vehicle for "willing God's will:"

Picturing God must precede any speaking about God, for our pictures accompany all our words and they continue long after we fall silent before God.
Ann Belford Ulanov

Relax and breathe gently. Become aware of God's presence, imaging it as light and warmth. Allow this Shekinah (glory) to fill your consciousness.

When we are in God's presence we are not alone. We are there with all God's children held in the divine embrace. Choose one of those children who has a need for healing of body, mind, or heart.

Lift this person into God's light. Visualize God's love bathing the person, and gently penetrating defenses, dissolving pain, cleansing wounds. Use any images that seem appropriate: dark becoming light, ice melting, confusion ordered.

See the person in a state of wholeness in God's light, newly created, fresh and beautiful as seen through the eyes of divine love.

Ask God that this beauty be fully realized according to God's design for this person. Thank God for whatever gift of healing is given. Release the person into God's care until you pray again.

This exercise can tutor you to use your imagination more actively in other prayers: visualize restored relationships; "see" old animosities dissolve. You are not trying to manufacture results, but envisioning with God the restoration of creation.

Write Your Own Psalm

This exercise can help you become more aware of your feelings in relation to God, and give you permission to express them in prayer. If you have held on to feelings like grief, anger, or a desire for revenge, believing it would be dangerous to express them to God, try writing your own prayer in psalm form:

Select a psalm that voices the feelings you are afraid to speak (Pss. 13, 22, 42, 77, 88, and 94 are possibilities). Ask God to help you accept the reality of your feelings.

Get acquainted with this psalm, especially the verses that best express your attitudes.

Lay it aside and begin to write your own psalm to God. Let it emerge from your experience, your feelings, and your faith.

Be as honest as you can.

If you want your feelings to change, include that desire in your psalm. If you find your feelings changing as you express them to God, include the changes of heart, too. You may end with a different perspective than you began with.

Offer your personal psalm to God as heartfelt prayer, asking the Spirit to take your feelings in a direction that will be for your healing and God's glory.

Paraphrase a Psalm

A related exercise is to paraphrase a psalm by putting yourself into it personally. Use the psalm structure, but simplify and modify the words to make it express your own experience. Here is a simplified example, based on Psalm 44 (a national lament):

> I have heard with my ears, O God,
> what deeds you performed in the days of old.
> Yet you have rejected and abased me.
> You have made me the taunt of my relatives,
> the laughing stock of my neighbors.
> All this has come upon me,
> yet I have not forgotten you.
> Why do you forget my affliction and misery?
> Come to my help, for the sake of your love!

Write a Conversation

Another exercise is to write a dialogue with a person from scripture. The following example imagines Jesus as a conversation partner; the writer is identifying with Simon Peter after the miraculous catch of fish (Luke 5:1–11).

ME: Go away from me, Lord, for I am a sinful person!

JESUS: Don't be afraid; from now on you will be catching people.

M: No, you don't understand, Lord. You are holy, pure. I'm just a common person with a lot of weaknesses. I don't belong with you.

J: Remember, you didn't choose me, I chose you.

M: But why, Lord? I'm not worthy of you!

J: Did I say you had to be worthy? I only ask you to follow me in trust.

As you can see, dialogue like this goes beyond the scripture story to become part of one's own faith story. You don't need to worry about whether or not it is really what Jesus would have said. The responses that come to mind as you write the dialogue become a vehicle of self-discovery in relation to God. And you may arrive at new insights into scripture as well as greater self-knowledge. This is as it should be, for prayer is a process of discovering ourselves more fully in God's love.

We have been discussing aspects of *communication* in prayer, and exercises that can help us communicate more freely with God. Now it is time to look at a deeper level of prayer that I call *communion*.

Prayer as Communion

My commonest attitude is this simple attentiveness, an habitual, loving turning of my eyes to God.
Brother Lawrence

When I speak of *communion*, I mean that dimension of relationship that goes beyond words, images, or actions. Communion transcends the particularities of communication. Just as listening and speaking are the primary expressions of prayer as communication, contemplation is the foremost expression of prayer as communion.

Contemplative Prayer

A simple gaze toward One who loves us unshakably—this is contemplative prayer. It is absorption in loving God with our whole being—not strenuously, but as a spontaneous response of the heart. Contemplative prayer is resting in God, allowing the Spirit to fill and move us as God wills. It is pure receptivity and adoration. It is quiet, tender, and sober, or playful, gentle, and joyous.

Contemplative prayer has the quality of an inner Sabbath. In a world driven by the need to accomplish and acquire, in a world where we judge one another on the basis of performance, God calls us to the radical trust of rest. Does the Lord require so much of us that we cannot join God in a little divine rest?

The late Russian Orthodox archbishop Anthony Bloom tells of an eighteenth-century priest who once asked an aged peasant what he was doing during the hours and hours he spent sitting in the chapel. The old man replied, "I look at Him, He looks at me, and we are happy."[7]

A more homely illustration of contemplation was recently recounted by a Protestant pastor who had returned from a visit to a monastery. He confessed to his son that he did not understand how the monks could sit for hours in the chapel before the Reserved Host (consecrated bread that represents the presence of Christ). His son, whose wife had just given birth to their first child, responded, "You know Dad, I think I understand. Since our newborn arrived, I just go to her crib and look at her. She doesn't have to do a thing, she doesn't even have to be awake. I am so utterly fascinated that I don't know where the time goes!"

This new father experienced contemplation in its natural sense: total absorption in what we see, like a child wholly concentrated in play.[8] It is an experience of being present only to the moment, unconscious of time. Deep contemplation draws us momentarily into the eternal realm that transcends time.

We gazed, enravished, you and I,
Like children at a flower.
            Walter de la Mare

In contemplation we move from communicating with God through speech to communing with God through the gaze of love. Words fall away, and the most palpable reality is being present to the lover of our souls. When we let go of all effort to speak or even to listen, simply becoming quiet before God, the Spirit is free to work its healing mysteries in us: releasing us from bondage, energizing new patterns of life, restoring our soul's beauty. Here we allow ourselves to be loved by God into wholeness.

Such communion with God is an end in itself, not a means to another end, however good. We do not enter the prayer of rest in order to become better servants of God; that is a natural side effect. The sole purpose of contemplation is to adore and enjoy God, which glorifies divine love. The first article of the Westminster Shorter Catechism asks what our chief end as human beings is. The response is that we are to glorify and enjoy God forever! Do we ever stop to think what it means to *enjoy* God?

Why do we have such trouble believing that God longs for our companionship and delights in it, just as the Lord enjoyed "walking in the cool of the day" with Adam and Eve in a young creation? What will it take to convince us that God also yearns for *us* to delight in the divine presence? Part of our spiritual maturation is learning to love God for who God is, not only for what God does for us.

Invitations to Explore

Perhaps it is only by giving ourselves to contemplative prayer and rest that we discover such truths for ourselves. Several pathways of prayer can lead you into an experience of Christian contemplation. I have chosen to focus on two basic forms: prayer of presence and prayer of the heart. Under prayer of the heart I describe three distinct methods: the Jesus Prayer, centering prayer, and breath prayer. The prayer of presence and breath prayer are presented as step-by-step exercises, as they seem especially practical and adaptable to the busy lives most of us lead.

Prayer of Presence

Find a posture that allows you to be relaxed and alert. It helps to have your neck and spine aligned. Close your eyes and breathe deeply several times. Consciously release any muscle tension you become aware of. Breathe in peace, breathe out tension.

You may find it easier to try this kind of prayer with someone else guiding you through it at a gentle pace. Consider taping the instructions, timing it in a way that seems comfortable so you will be free to enter the process without having to read it. Or, you may simply familiarize yourself with the content before praying at your own leisure.

Relax your mind. If particular thoughts keep returning, gather them up and give them to God to hold for you during this time. You can take them back later if you want.

Turn your attention to God's presence. Let yourself be fully aware of the mystery of divine love that continually surrounds and upholds us. God is breathing life into you at each moment; take in the gift.

Let God's presence fill your consciousness, and simply rest in this presence—just as you might with someone you love dearly and feel no need to speak to, just to be with. Let yourself be like a child cradled in the lap of a wonderful parent or grandparent; or perhaps gently supported in an ocean of light; or enfolded in a peaceful warmth. Let yourself be held in God's tender embrace; rest and soak up the love that holds you.

Close your prayer by thanking God for any gifts received in this time. You can return to this communion of presence whenever you choose to receive it.

Surely God's heart is comforted when we take seriously the love that is offered us, when we are willing to receive what God longs to give us! How would a mother feel if her child resisted every expression of the overwhelming tenderness in her heart? How would a father feel if his child ran off at any sign of affection? Yet we seem so often willing to leave God lonely and disconsolate without us. Communion is *mutual* consolation and joy.

You may want to imagine your ideal parent. Scripture urges us to recognize God's parental care for us. If this is difficult because of personal history, there is no need to force any particular image. Let the Spirit guide you to an image that allows you to know the enfolding love of God. If you have trouble allowing God to love you, remember this: There is nothing you can do to make God love you more, and although there are things you can do to grieve God, there is nothing you can do to make God love you less! Relax and let yourself receive the reality of God's eternal love.

Prayer of the Heart

There is a long history of Christian prayer that aims to move us "from head to heart." Remember that this means moving from a limited and partial dimension of our lives to the center of our whole being. Prayers of the heart are typified by short phrases. They are repeated first on the lips and then in the mind, until they take on a life of their own deep within us. When such prayers become embedded in our life awareness and daily activity, they have truly become "heart prayers."

The oldest of these prayers, known as the "Jesus Prayer," combines the prayer of the tax collector from Luke 18:13 ("God, be merciful to me, a sinner") with the earliest confession of the Christian church ("Jesus is Lord"). The long form is, "Lord Jesus Christ, Son of the living God, have mercy on me, a sinner." The short form is "Lord, have mercy" (*kyrie eleison*). Consistent use of this prayer has been, for many, a path to the contemplation of Christ and communion with the risen Lord.

Accustom yourself to walk in the presence of God. . . . To preserve this remembrance, choose a few short prayers . . . and repeat them often with appropriate thoughts and feelings.

Theophan the Recluse

A way of prayer closely related to this ancient form is now enjoying a revival among Christians of several traditions. It is called "centering prayer," and is a good way to introduce the person in the pew to contemplation. Centering prayer is based on a fourteenth-century treatise titled *The Cloud of Unknowing*. In this way of prayer, you select a single word that sums up for you the nature and being of God. Single-minded focus on this prayer word in silent concentration becomes a vehicle into the mystery of divine presence and grace. The method bears a striking resemblance to Eastern meditation with mantras but has developed independently out of the mystical strands of Western Christianity.[9]

The practice of the Jesus Prayer is simple. Stand before the Lord with the attention in the heart, and call to Him: "Lord Jesus Christ, Son of God, have mercy on me!" The essential part of this is not in the words, but in faith, contrition, and self-surrender to the Lord. With these feelings one can stand before the Lord even without any words, and it will still be prayer.

Theophan the Recluse

A contemporary version of the Jesus Prayer is called "breath prayer" because the words for breath and spirit are the same in Hebrew (*ruach*) and the use of this kind of prayer over time helps us experience what it means for the Spirit to pray in us (Rom. 8:26–27). It is also a short prayer that can be said or thought in a single breath. As a prayer of the heart, it is especially easy to learn and practice. Ron DelBene, an Episcopal priest who developed this method from the older tradition, suggests that you find your own prayer of the heart.[10] One way to do so is to:

> Visualize Jesus standing before you, asking you: "(*your name*), what do you want me to do for you?" Let your response surface from deep within. If more than one thing comes to mind, identify the root desire beneath all the others.

Sample breath prayers:
Holy Spirit, fill me.
Give me strength, O Christ.
Father, show me your love.
Teach me patience, gracious God.
My God and my All. (Saint Francis)
Come, Lord Jesus!

Next, identify how you normally address God in prayer: Lord, Jesus, Holy One, Living Spirit, Eternal God? Find your name for the divine being.

Combine your desire with your name for God in a single short phrase that flows easily in your mind. You may need to experiment with phrasing to find a comfortable rhythm.

Sit quietly and repeat the phrase gently in your mind for several minutes. Take a walk, repeating your prayer while you move. Note how the prayer shapes your perceptions. You can carry this prayer with you through the day. It fits well with many solitary activities from common household chores and routine tasks to standing in line and sitting in traffic jams! It is a good companion for rhythmic exercise such as walking, jogging, or swimming as well.

Samples of scripture and hymn phrases:
Glory to God in the highest!
My soul magnifies the Lord.
Be still and know that I am God.
Create in me a clean heart, O God.
Perfect love casts out fear.
Lo, I am with you always.
Be Thou my vision, O Lord of my heart.
Come, my Way, my Truth, my Life.
Jesus, priceless treasure.

Scripture and hymn phrases can be prayed in the same way. Many of us have committed to memory a few verses of scripture that are particularly precious. We turn to them in times of special need or irrepressible joy. Simple tunes often help to carry our prayer phrase for us.

Repeated prayers tend to deepen and expand in meaning as they are used in various contexts of life. Over time, the repetition creates a space in which words fall away and we become more aware of the Presence they point to.

Simple objects or images can also be the focus of contemplative prayer. A single flower, leaf, or candle may become a pointer to divine presence. In the Eastern Orthodox Church, icons (images of Christ, Mary, and the saints) are a focus of contemplation. Henri Nouwen's book *Behold the Beauty of the Lord* is a helpful introduction to contemplation with icons.[11]

I have been describing methods of contemplation that use words and images. Yet every form of contemplative prayer aims to draw us past words and images to that mysterious place where God dwells in gracious union with the human soul.

> *Whereas St. Benedict, who has set the tone for the spirituality of the West, calls us first of all to listen, the Byzantine fathers focus on gazing. . . . Icons are painted to lead us into the inner room of prayer and bring us close to the heart of God.*
> *Henri J. M. Nouwen*

Practical Matters

The discussion of prayer would be incomplete without some attention to very practical matters such as time, place, and the irritation of distractions.

There is no substitute for giving time to the practice of prayer. Like most things, we learn best by doing it. But the issue of time is a formidable barrier for many of us. We live in a culture that equates constant activity and meaning. Time is often the "commodity" we are least willing to give up without tangible compensation. We all make choices about our use of time. The way we use time reveals our priorities, much as we might like to think otherwise. If I were to learn that I had only six months to live, my use of time would no doubt change significantly!

> *The great thing is prayer. Prayer itself. If you want a life of prayer, the way to get it is by praying. . . . You start where you are and you deepen what you already have.*
> *Thomas Merton*

If our relationship with God is really important to us, we will make time to pray. It might mean going to bed earlier in order to get up earlier. It might mean taking a portion of our lunch hour for solitude. It could involve swapping child care with a friend for a period each day. It certainly means claiming the time that is thrust upon us when we are sick or delayed in travel. Most of us could learn to waste less time over inconsequential matters so that we have more time for what is important. Developing the habit of regular prayer is like building any new habit into our life: it takes firm commitment, creativity, and perseverance.

None of this will happen unless we *desire* a deeper relationship with God. Desire for God is fuel for prayer. When we fall in love, we readily set other things aside in order to secure coveted time to be with our beloved. It should be no different with God.

In choosing a time for prayer, it is important to take personal rhythms into account. Some of us are morning persons, some are night owls, and some experience peak energy at midday. God deserves some of the best time of our day, not the dregs.

It is easier, especially for beginners, to pay attention to God in solitude and relative quiet. For some, this poses a creative challenge. I have known people who took early morning walks in New York's Central Park for prayer. Others have learned to shut out the noise around them by entering the inner sanctuary of their heart. Some families identify a particular chair that entitles its occupant to quiet and solitude. Some have turned a spare closet into a literal "prayer closet."

When you have found your place for prayer, sanctify it through frequent use. Make it sacred space. You may want to arrange a few symbols of divine presence and beauty in it. Remember, you are not a disembodied spirit. Pay attention to your body; bring it into your prayer so it can be a support rather than a distraction. Give yourself permission to experiment with postures and gestures.

Finally, there is the matter of distractions that inevitably surface in prayer. Outside distractions are easier to handle (see chap. 2). When the noises of civilization or nature intrude, as they invariably do despite our best efforts to find or create solitude, it is best simply to accept them and return to your prayer intentions.

Inner distractions are more difficult. Saints through the centuries have offered colorful descriptions of how the mind, left to its own devices, functions: "like monkeys jumping around in banana trees," or a "swarm of mosquitoes" buzzing in all directions. The psychological term is "free association." This is precisely why you need simple words, phrases, or images to help you concentrate on God's presence. Remember that certain kinds of prayer—prayers of thanksgiving, confession, or supplication—give the mind a train of thought to focus on, whereas listening prayer and contemplation tend to generate more inner distraction.

Be prepared for distractions and be patient with them. If you try to fight them head-on, the attention will make them stronger. Better to simply note that you have wandered from your focus, and gently return your attention to God. Persistent thoughts may require closer examination. Do they represent something you need to confess, a person you need to be reconciled to, a situation that calls for your response? There is a Jewish tradition that

I can be praying and find my mind on another matter, . . . on someone who has hurt me, on a problem coming up. This kind of distraction indicates what is . . . not integrated into my personal relationship with Jesus Christ. . . . I can put the matter into his hands, turning the distraction into a prayer.

Robert L. Faricy

50

sees distractions in prayer as "blemished deeds in our lives that crowd their way into the time of prayer in expectation of a blessing."[12] Might this be true for you?

The most important thing is to keep praying, even if it feels artificial at first. Expect to learn in the process. Experiment with different forms of prayer, but keep a balance between thanksgiving and supplication, confession and intercession, speaking and listening, communication and communion. God will bless whatever offering you make from the heart with commitment and sincerity. The more you give yourself to prayer, the more life you will find in it.

Notes

1. John S. Mogabgab, unpublished writings.
2. Richard J. Foster, *Celebration of Discipline* (New York: Harper & Row, 1978), 16.
3. Douglas V. Steere, *Dimensions of Prayer* (New York: Women's Division, Board of Global Ministries of the United Methodist Church, 1962).
4. From the *Epistle to Diognetus*, cited in Steere's *Dimensions of Prayer*, 19, 23.
5. Attributed to Jane Edwards; source unknown.
6. These insights are borrowed from Steere, *Dimensions of Prayer*, 82–83.
7. Anthony Bloom, *Beginning to Pray* (New York: Paulist Press, 1970), 62.
8. I maintain a distinction between "natural contemplation," such as the complete absorption of a viewer in a glorious sunset (which may or may not be experienced as a medium of God's presence) and "Christian contemplation," which involves a direct experience of the presence of God unmediated by thoughts, images, or physical senses.
9. Father Thomas Keating, who has written and taught extensively on centering prayer, believes this resemblance is superficial. See his *Open Mind, Open Heart* (Rockport, Mass.: Element, 1992).
10. See any one of several short and very accessible books by Ron DelBene with Herb Montgomery, such as *The Breath of Life, The Hunger of the Heart,* and *Into the Light* (Upper Room Books).
11. Henri J. M. Nouwen, *Behold the Beauty of the Lord* (Notre Dame, Ind.: Ave Maria Press, 1987).
12. Steere, *Dimensions of Prayer*, 40.

4 Gathered in the Spirit
Our Common Worship

> My whole heart I lay upon the altar of thy praise, an
> whole burnt-offering of praise I offer to thee. . . . Let
> the flame of thy love . . . set on fire my whole heart,
> let nought in me be left to myself, nought wherein I
> may look to myself, but may I wholly burn towards
> thee, wholly be on fire toward thee, wholly love thee,
> as though set on fire by thee.
>
> Saint Augustine

Christian philosopher Søren Kierkegaard developed an analogy
called "the theater of worship." It invites us to see public worship
as a kind of theater performance, and asks us to identify the stage,
actors, and audience. Based on our experience of worship, most
of us would probably locate the stage in the church chancel and
see worship leaders as the actors performing for a congregational
audience. But Kierkegaard asks us to see the sanctuary as a stage
on which the entire congregation acts, prompted by ministers and
musicians. The audience is God!

The word *liturgy* comes from the Greek *leitourgia*, which simply means the service or work of the people. Worship is the work
of all the faithful who gather to praise, honor, and glorify God.
Have you ever thought about what kind of *service* to God a "worship service" is? Acts of service to one another have a sacrificial
character. We serve God when worship expresses a spirit of sacrifice: first a sacrifice of praise and thanksgiving, then a complete
self-offering—a willingness to listen for God's Word and to give
ourselves wholly to God's designs in the world. We offer our will,
strength, and gifts in gratitude for who God is and what God has
done for us.

Of course, it is also true that in worship we are served by God.
God fills us with the joy of knowing we are loved, restores our
courage through forgiveness, provides the Word for hungry

laos—the people (laity)
ourgia—service or work

hearts, and fills us with the bread and wine of new life in Christ, giving new purpose to our lives. From this perspective, the stage of worship is the very kingdom of God, the prime actor is the Holy Spirit, and we—leaders and people alike—are the audience. Christian worship is paradoxical. God is both the audience and the main actor. We too are both actors and audience.

Our worship is rooted in who God is and in God's purposes. We worship because it is natural to respond to the mystery that irradiates life. We know God to be holy and pure, just and true, compassionate and loving. God is worthy to receive our praise and acclaim, worthy of our listening ears and offered hearts. The "worth-ship" of God is the origin of human worship! We also worship because we are created to reflect and glorify the One in whose image we are made. Eastern Christians believe we are most truly ourselves when we glorify God, finding our "perfection and fulfillment in worship."[1]

Worship ushers us into the presence of the living God and demands the attention, receptivity, and response of our whole being. It asks us to disengage from the nose-length focus of daily life and see below the surface to life's source. We can then reengage the realities of the world from a deeper and clearer perspective.

Worship from the Heart

"You shall love the Lord your God with all your heart, and with all your soul, and with all your mind, and with all your strength" (Mark 12:29–30). When Jesus identifies this great commandment, he sets worship at the center of human life. Worship, as full-hearted love of God, is meant to permeate our lives. Private or public, it is always first and foremost a matter of the heart.

We cannot realize the richness and vitality of worship until we comprehend the meaning of *heart* in the Judeo-Christian tradition. In Western culture, *head* and *heart* describe separate spheres. *Head* signifies our rational, analytic functions while *heart* represents our feeling capacities. But a purely emotional heart does not express its scriptural significance.

In the Jewish tradition, the heart is the seat and center of the whole person, the core of personal character, including thought, emotion, will, intuition, and imagination. Thoughts, both good and evil, arise from the heart; motives, desires, and intentions come

To worship is to quicken the conscience by the holiness of God, to feed the mind with the truth of God, to purge the imagination by the beauty of God, to open the heart to the love of God, to devote the will to the purpose of God.

William Temple

from the heart. When the heart is turned toward God, one is filled with grace and truth; when the heart turns away, a person dwells in delusion. The Christian church inherited this understanding of "heart" from the Jewish tradition.

True worship from the heart, then, means responding to God's glory and love with our entire being. After all, when Spirit touches spirit, we are *moved*—both in feelings and commitments. Too many worshiping communities encourage only half-hearted worship. In churches that tend toward reason and order, many members yearn to express the intuitive and feeling side of faith. In churches where intellect is considered a poor cousin to emotional experiences of faith, many people are hungry for serious study and responsible action. Many Protestant churches of European background tend to neglect the body and its senses in worship; churches with African and Hispanic roots tend to include the body in celebrations of worship. Part of the gift of our increasingly multicultural society is the opportunity to learn various styles of worship from one another, and to appreciate the gifts of each tradition.

Worship from the heart joins inner reality with outward expression. Reciting words and doing rituals may be important training in the faith, but will not finally satisfy the soul. Personal integrity demands more than external form: "these people draw near with their mouths and honor me with their lips, while their hearts are far from me, and their worship of me is a human commandment learned by rote" (Isa. 29:13). Yet such integrity cannot be produced by a simple act of will on our part. As author Richard Foster reminds us, "Until God touches and frees our spirit we cannot enter this realm. . . . Our spirit must be ignited by the divine fire."[2]

In African-American culture the emotional is not the opposite of the spiritual, nor is there any separation between the emotional and the intellectual. Both the mind and the heart are needed to grasp the truth.
Jamie Phelps

Save me from the soothing sin
Of the empty cultic deed
And the pious, babbling din
Of the claimed but unlived creed.
Let my actions, Lord, express
What my tongue and lips profess.
Thomas H. Troeger
©Oxford University Press, Inc.

The Need to Gather

For many people, private worship is more attractive than public worship. Envisioning faith as a private affair reflects the individualism of our culture. Many ask why corporate worship should be so important when they can meditate on God in nature with far less distraction, or why they should bother to get dressed up and go to church when they can listen to an inspiring message on radio or TV.

The reasons for gathering are many and important. Whether we are alone or with others, we need to experience our Christian life as rooted in the larger community of faith. Even our most personal disciplines need to be supported, broadened, clarified, and sometimes corrected in the light of corporate theology and practice. Otherwise we become susceptible to privatized visions of spiritual truth. Moreover, we need the prayers of others as they need our prayers. The way God provides for our deepest hopes is usually through the hands and hearts of others.

While a worshipful attitude should permeate one's entire life, the role of common worship is crucial. We delude ourselves if we imagine we can live the spiritual life in total isolation from Christian community, for it is impossible to be Christian in solitary splendor. To be Christian is to be joined to the Body of Christ. The central and visible way in which the church expresses this reality is by gathering in the Spirit to receive and respond to God's living Word.

We gather for worship to remember who and whose we are. We come to recount the stories that shape our faith, stories that turn us from a collection of individuals into a community with a common source and vision. The church as a worshiping community carries our biblical faith and spiritual tradition down through the ages to each individual. We are joined to that community in Baptism, tutored in faith through the interpretation of scripture in preaching, and nourished at the Lord's Table *as a family of believers.* Life in the church teaches us that we are made for communion not only with God but with one another in Christ.

Without the rites and sacraments of public worship, there would be no Body of Christ. It is through the praises, prayers, sacraments, and scriptural proclamations of common worship that the church is continually given its life. In this respect, worship is the most fundamental of all Christian practices.

Common worship leads us through the seasons of Jesus' life and the life of the early church. Every time we move through Advent, Christmas, Lent, Easter, and Pentecost, we are given fresh occasion to take to heart the meaning of Jesus' life in relation to our own. Each year allows us to reexperience the coming of the Messiah, the Lord's risen presence, the birth of the church and the energy of her mission. Such knowledge is impossible to come by on our own, even if we are steeped in the Bible. How can we

Indeed, liturgy continually confronts us with the call to sacrifice our preoccupation with self. Because liturgy is intrinsically corporate, it resists any narrowing of the spiritual life to a private relationship between the solitary soul and God. Liturgy places God in the center and us in community.

John S. Mogabgab

People gathered for genuine worship "are like a heap of fresh and burning coals warming one another as a great strength, freshness and vigor of life flows into all."

Isaac Pennington

comprehend the significance of Pentecost if we do not experience the grace of the Holy Spirit in a living community of faith? How can we understand the mission of the church if we are isolated from the church?

Finally, worship in community means that we can present a united front "against the cosmic powers of this present darkness" (Eph. 6:12). Biblical scholar Walter Wink argues eloquently that the powers and principalities of this world are corporate in nature.[3] It takes a *communal* witness of light, truth, and peace to overcome the corporate power of darkness, deception, and destruction in this world.

Of course, we need to keep in mind that there are faithful members of the Body of Christ who are committed to the importance of common worship but are physically unable to come. Frail, elderly people and those who are homebound, the physically disabled whose churches are inaccessible, call the gathered community to accountability. Television or radio broadcasts of worship may be a blessing to such persons. But even more important are the ways their fellow members bring community to them in their particular circumstances. Pastors providing home Communion to shut-ins is a fairly standard practice, but greater creativity is called for in bringing community to the faithful with limited mobility. Giving homebound parishioners ways to connect to the larger community can be accomplished in several ways: for example, they can be given a special mission of prayer for the pastors and congregation; those who are able can be included in outreach through writing or craft projects; and they can form community with one another through prayer, phone calls, and letters.[4] Congregations need to give more attention to this matter.

Do you think forced isolation makes a person more conscious of the gift and importance of common worship? What might we learn from persons in such circumstances?

Keeping Sabbath

Christian worship is a way of "remembering the sabbath day to keep it holy" (Exod. 20:8). Holy means "set apart." In keeping the Sabbath, we set aside specific time to respond to the wonder and beauty of One who is present in all time, to acknowledge and bless our living Source.

For Christians, the grace and truth of God have been decisively revealed in the death and resurrection of Jesus. Since Christ's resurrection took place on the first day of the week, Christians have called that day the Lord's Day. Every Sunday is a "little Easter," so Christian worship is essentially a celebration of new life in Christ.

It is a sign forever between me and the people of Israel that in six days the Lord made heaven and earth, and on the seventh day [God] rested, and was refreshed.

Exod. 31:17

Like the Jewish Sabbath, the Lord's Day is understood to be an opportunity to rest from ordinary labor and activity. Indeed, we are *commanded* to rest on the Sabbath. All the divine commands are life-giving. God knows we need rest and provides us with a personal example to follow. The Sabbath command is really an invitation to participate in *God's* rest, as renowned biblical scholar Walter Brueggemann acknowledges:

> The commandment looks back to the rest of God. . . . God's governance is not one of anxiety or franticness. The world is confidently, serenely ordered as God's good creation . . . [and] the goal and crown of life in the community of covenant is the freedom, space, and delight of sabbath rest. In keeping sabbath rest, the human community . . . participates in the tranquillity God has ordained into the structure of creation.[5]

The Sabbath command is especially relevant to contemporary life. How difficult it is for people in our achievement- and production-obsessed culture to rest. Keeping the Sabbath means trusting God to be God, recognizing that we are not indispensable. When we refuse to take a single day a week for genuine refreshment and rest, we try to outdo even God! In the light of God's rest, our anxious, compulsive activities may be exposed as little more than efforts to stay in control, or to fabricate life's meaning out of constant activity.

O God of the Sabbath, I work too much. Work is good and necessary and I thank you for it, but I need to play more. I need to rest and relax, to walk and run, see friends and enjoy myself. Remind me, God, to take time off, and help me not to feel guilty when I do.

Avery Brooke

The purpose of Sabbath rest is to free us inwardly for full-hearted worship. Genuine worship flows from a heart that trusts God to uphold the universe. The joy and peace of worship come from entrusting ourselves to divine provision, and releasing ourselves from the illusion that labor is the chief source of our life—even if that labor is for the church or felt to be an expression of God's will! Rest and worship are expressions of deep trust.

What, in your experience, makes it difficult to "keep the Sabbath"? Cultural factors? Personal habits or attitudes? Make a list below, and add to it as you discover new reasons.

Each of us needs "mini Sabbaths" in the course of a given day, as well as extended Sabbaths for deeper "re-creation." But the weekly day set apart to keep Sabbath with our faith community remains the foundation and model for other kinds of Sabbath rest.

Worship as Problem

Unfortunately, many people find corporate worship a source of frustration rather than fulfillment. Our actual experience on Sunday morning may embody few of the realities I have described, even if we believe in them. We may feel that we are neither actors nor audience before God, but passive (and not always happy) recipients of the limited worship forms of particular churches and their leaders.

Perhaps we come seeking a lively community of faith, and find people who seem bored, preoccupied, uninterested in visitors, or eager to escape from Christian fellowship for Sunday brunch and afternoon golf. Perhaps we feel unable to penetrate the circles of people who seem to be at the heart of the church's life. We may find ourselves unaccepted for a variety of reasons, including any form of brokenness in our personal life. We may consistently leave worship feeling isolated and lonely.

Perhaps we come to hear a word of life in the scriptures and to receive edification in the preached word, but are subjected to passages rendered meaningless, dull, or exaggerated by the manner in which they are read. There may be neither time nor inner space offered to *hear* God's Word. We may be dished up a heavy dose of ideology, the preacher's personal views, or endless anecdotes strung together and passed off as a sermon. Maybe the preacher speaks down to us, harangues us, or fails to connect the sermon to our daily experience of life. We become weary and angry instead of energized with good news.

Perhaps we come with an eagerness to sing the great hymns of our faith, hymns we may have known by heart from childhood. We may find a new hymnal with tunes that seem unsingable, or familiar tunes with unfamiliar words that leave us confused and dissatisfied.

Perhaps we have been growing in our prayer life and have a strong desire to contribute our prayers to those of the gathered community. We may find no space in the service for our prayers. They may all be printed or spoken on our behalf, although they do not express what is in our heart.

We may hunger for a deeper sacramental experience in our worship. Many Protestants from nonsacramental traditions (Presbyterian, Methodist, Baptist, Congregational) have begun exploring the spiritual riches of the larger catholic church

Has your worship experience changed for the better or worse over the years? Are there aspects of your worship experience that seem consistently unsatisfying to you? If so, name them below.

(Anglican, Roman Catholic, Eastern Orthodox) through private retreats or ecumenical training programs. We may return to our churches with an acute sense of loss where the sacraments are concerned, especially Holy Communion. There is neither the frequency of celebration we may crave, nor the sense of spiritual depth and mystery we have come to respect. An expectation of the real, risen presence of Christ often seems absent in our worship experience.

Other sources of dissatisfaction abound. We may yearn for greater freedom of expression in posture, gesture, and movement. We may thirst for periods of silence to balance the barrage of words. We may crave the visual blessing of beauty, light, color, and richness of symbol. We may feel that public worship has little "heart" or integrity at all. Perhaps it feels ever more rote and external each Sunday. When God seems remote, worship will feel as dry as the Sahara. We come for living water and leave with unquenched thirst. We come to be nourished and leave with a mouthful of sand.

Not everyone experiences such inadequacy in public worship, nor in all these forms at once! Yet as people become hungrier for spiritual nurture, they often become more dissatisfied with their own tradition of corporate worship. Part of the problem is that the average person in the pew has little say over how worship is planned, much less over how leaders read, preach, and pray.

How, then, are we to become lively actors in the drama of human worship before God? How can we be better attuned to God in spite of the foibles of worship leaders, the frailties of worshiping communities, and the inadequacies of our own feelings and judgments?

Worship as Promise: Practices for Deepening Our Worship

Worship need not be completely determined by the limitations of human leaders or communities. There are things we can do to help enliven our experience of common worship. We may have little power to change the external forms, but we can certainly change our way of entering into worship. We can take responsibility for our own experience in three important ways: by preparing in advance for the Sunday service; by engaging worship itself with a different quality of awareness; and by taking the initiative to speak with worship planners and leaders about how we experience worship.

Preparation

The single most important thing we can do to change our experience of public worship is to revitalize our practice of personal worship. In earlier times the weekly prayers of the gathered community were nurtured by the daily prayers of faithful families and individuals, just as a river is fed by smaller streams. Now that is rarely the case. Small wonder, then, if public worship feels spiritually dry and unappealing.

When we begin to steep ourselves in scripture on a regular basis, we hear the Sunday scripture readings differently. Our own daily prayer becomes tilled soil for receiving the seed of God's Word in the liturgy. The practice of *Lectio Divina* is ideal for personal prayer, as are any of the prayer practices discussed in chapter 3. Morning and evening prayer have been the classic "daily offices" of personal and family worship in the Protestant tradition. They generally include at least a psalm, a New Testament reading, a song, and a few prayers, although the number of elements can be adapted as needed. Committing to even one such practice daily will immeasurably enrich our experience of common worship.

Christians have always known that public worship—particularly the celebration of the sacraments—requires inward preparation. It was at one time common practice to examine oneself through prayer and confession before participating in the Sunday service. If we spend half an hour assessing our life before God, either Saturday evening or early Sunday morning, we will discover a natural bridge between our personal prayer and common worship. We will find unexpected connections between our life experience and the words of the liturgy, and we will deepen our receptivity to the grace of Word and Sacrament.

Many people have found it enriching to prepare for common worship as a group. A weekly Bible study focusing on the passage to be preached the following Sunday can bring the experience of worship to life in a new way. When we have studied the background of a text and reflected on how it speaks to our lives, we

The discipline of prayer can mightily weave the fabric of a congregation's liturgical life. And liturgy in turn can be to the people a "school of prayer."
Paul Hoon

Three excellent guides to daily prayer for individuals and families are:
Book of Common Worship: Daily Prayer *(Westminster/John Knox Press, 1993);* **A Guide to Prayer for Ministers and Other Servants** *(The Upper Room, 1983);* **A Guide to Prayer for All God's People** *(The Upper Room, 1990)*

Try out a half-hour self-examination (see chap. 6) this weekend, directing the following questions to God:

When have I been aware of your presence, guidance, or grace this week? How did I respond?

When have I been especially unaware of your presence, guidance, or grace this week? Why?

What habit of the heart do I need to acquire in order to live more faithfully?

61

are likely to find connections with the sermon regardless of its quality. Such study groups are easier to maintain over time if the preaching follows a lectionary, but if the passage is known in advance, topical preaching can also allow for a useful group process.

During Worship

Many find it helpful to arrive for worship ten minutes early in order to distance themselves from last-minute rushing and prepare themselves to worship God from the heart. This is a good time to pray for both worship leaders and worshipers, asking the Spirit to be actively present and known by the gathered community, and for the faithfulness and integrity of the church in its worship and mission.

Once the worship service has begun, you can do several things to heighten your awareness of God's presence. First, be prepared to hear God speak—to you personally and to the whole gathering. Recognize that God can catch our attention through any part of the service, not only through the ways we expect. Pay attention to the meaning of the words in printed prayers and affirmations as you speak them. You don't have to let the congregational drone of unison reading dull your mind.

Listen to the words of hymns with an ear for the meaning of the sentences. Sometimes this meaning is obscured by musical phrases that do not correspond to the spoken phrase; some idioms in older hymns need explanation in order to make sense. But hymns are one of the richest sources of heartfelt worship in the Protestant tradition. They allow us to express depths of joy, praise, sorrow, and yearning in music as well as words, joining emotion and thought in profound unity. Anthems serve much the same purpose. We can join our hearts in self-offering with the choir, even when we cannot join our voices. Music often carries our spirit Godward when nothing else can. It may be as much a source of inspiration as well-spoken words.

Listen carefully to any Psalm you may recite. The Psalms give us a realistic voice for praise, anguish, yearning, confession—a way to reveal the depths of the human soul to God. If we allow it, the Psalter can school us in uninhibited prayer. Regular recitation of the Psalms gives us a repertoire of prayers known by heart that can anchor us during the gale winds of life.

Amazing Grace: Hymn Texts for Devotional Use *(Westminster John Knox Press) is a words-only compilation of hymns that is a useful resource for reflecting on the meaning of hymn texts.*

When in our music God is glorified, and adoration leaves no room for pride, it is as though the whole creation cried: Alleluia!
Fred Pratt Green

Amen!

If all the prayers in your service are printed or offered by worship leaders, find where you can add your inward assent or "amen!" to the words other have placed before you. Not every word will express your own heart before God, but some of them probably will. Be attentive to where the public prayers of the church stretch you to a new perception, or offer to God something you had perhaps not thought important. The prayers of the church can tutor us in a richer language of personal prayer.

If you are given an opportunity to pray silently, offer to God what you discover in your heart at the time. Perhaps you are distracted by a fretful child nearby; pray for the well-being of that child and all the church's children, indeed for the children of the world. Perhaps the Gospel reading helped you see how fearful you are of people who are different; pray for those who seem most different, and pray to be released from fear so you can be free to serve. Let the themes, images, insights, and feelings from worship itself inform your prayers.

Perhaps you bring individual concerns to worship that seem only distantly related to the gathered community. If you are praying daily at home, such personal concerns will not likely prevent you from praying on behalf of the wider world. Sometimes, however, these issues are so overwhelming and immediate that our minds and hearts are completely taken over by them. Then it is well to ask for the prayers of our companions in faith, allowing the community to carry us until we find enough strength and healing to look to the needs of others again.

If certain parts of the service do not speak to you, stay focused inwardly on the parts that do. Ponder in your heart those phrases or insights that communicate the presence and grace of God to you. Let yourself respond inwardly to the gifts you *are* given in the time of worship. But remember that what speaks to you may not make you comfortable. God often communicates grace through challenge!

Claim for yourself the freedom to respond to God in worship with the fullness of your being. If tears are a natural part of your response to God's grace, or a way of communicating your need to God, let yourself cry. If you hear a word that tickles you with humor or joy, let yourself laugh! If you couldn't agree more with what the preacher says, nod your head or murmur an assent. Instead of allowing the inhibitions of others to control you, offer

When the Rev. Benjamin Weir was held hostage for several years in Lebanon, his memory of the Psalms helped to sustain him. Do you have a reservoir of scriptural prayers that you know "by heart"? What inner resources do you draw on in trying circumstances?

the example of your freedom to others. We need permission to feel and to move in our worship life.

There is nothing forbidden about using simple gestures to express what is in your heart to God. What could be more natural? We use gestures when communicating with each other, so why not with God? You may not be prepared for deep bows or even kneeling as gestures of reverence and self-offering, but smaller gestures may prove valuable aids to the integrity of your worship. Many people find that simply opening the palms of their hands in prayer, while standing, sitting, or kneeling, helps them to focus on the meaning of that prayer. I find such a gesture very unobtrusive, yet it helps me know the reality of my prayer in a deeper way. Using the body can help prayer become an expression of more than our distractible minds. The freedom we find in personal prayer to use various gestures or postures may, over time, make a significant contribution to our public worship.

Finally, we can observe and reflect upon whatever symbols of faith there may be in our places of worship. Some churches have beautiful stained glass windows with images and symbols worth pondering. Some have bright banners, or wood carvings. Most churches feature the central symbol of Christian faith, the cross, in a prominent place. Many also keep a traditional chalice and paten, or pitchers and plates, on the Communion table. Some have baptismal fonts in visible positions. Meditating on the meaning of these images can enrich and deepen other parts of a particular service. On occasions when the words of worship seem dry or inaccessible, we may find our sermon in visual symbols.

The Spirit is free to speak to us in an infinite variety of ways. If you do not find God's Word where you expect to, keep your ears open for the unexpected!

Take five minutes to try this exercise:

Sitting with you arms and legs crossed, say the Lord's Prayer silently. Then, if you are able and comfortable, try it again on your knees with the palms of your hands open before you.

Did you experience a difference in the way you prayed, or how it felt? If so, describe the difference below. If not, don't worry. It may be that posture and gesture do not generally affect your experience of prayer.

Beyond Worship

Although you may not be in a position to make direct decisions about how worship is planned and led, you can make your hopes and desires known to those who are. Don't be afraid to talk with your pastor or worship committee about your experience of common worship.

If you feel a need for more silent reflection time in the service, say so. You can suggest when quiet reflection would be most helpful to you: before the service, after scripture readings or sermon, during prayers of confession or intercession. If you crave more frequent celebration of the Lord's Supper, let your leadership know. There may be others like you who could form the nucleus of an early Sunday or weekday evening Eucharist. If you want to explore prayers for healing in your faith community, say so; there is historical precedent for services of healing prayer with the anointing of oil, commonly connected to the Eucharist, that was called "the medicine of immortality" by the early church.

Your suggestions need not be in the form of complaint, which may elicit defensiveness on the part of decision makers. They can be expressed as changes you yearn for that would enrich your experience of worship.

For Worship Leaders

If you are a worship leader or planner, there are many aspects of worship that only you can affect. The overall integrity of the service is your responsibility. The ordering of parts and the thematic unity of hymns, prayers, scripture, preaching, and sacraments belong to you. You can affect elements of worship that will have a significant impact on the congregation's experience of corporate prayer and praise.

Consider, for example, where time is allowed for silent reflection in the service as a whole. Silence helps clear away the static and clutter that impede our access to deeper thought. It leaves us free to pay attention to the presence of the One we have come to encounter in worship. In the services you lead, do people have a chance to reflect on the reality of God's presence in their midst? Are they given space to assimilate the messages proclaimed in scripture and preaching? Is time offered for silent prayers of confession or intercession?

Scripture reading in worship is often undervalued and one of the weakest elements of the service instead of one of the strongest. Pay attention to how Bible passages are read in your church. Does the reader convey a genuine understanding of what he or she is reading? Is the passage read without artificial emphases, sing-song phrasing, or unnatural exaggeration? Readers, including trained church professionals, need to practice scripture reading in advance of any service.

Ponder the place of our physical senses in worship. Space, light, symbol, sound, fragrance, and sacred art can be powerful vehicles for the experience of the holy. Assess your sanctuary: where does it express sensory beauty or sacred signs? Assess your worship service: how much of the whole person does it invite to participate in worship? Is there anything beyond words to encourage reflection on the goodness and beauty of God? There is a difference between simplicity and sterility.

Does the worship you plan take account of the fact that we are embodied creatures? Consider how your people participate physically in worship. What kinds of postures, gestures, or movement are encouraged? Are there occasions when the congregation can come forward to present special offerings (or to receive Communion in churches that typically partake seated)? Are particular gestures ever suggested for "passing the peace"? Some people are more comfortable with hand contact than with hugs, but shaking hands has a formal and secular significance that may lead us to feel we're saying "Hello, how are you?" rather than passing the peace of Christ. Creativity and imagination are called for here. I mentioned opening the palms of the hands when saying the Lord's Prayer. Another natural opportunity for movement occurs during the opening of the Eucharistic liturgy. When the celebrant says "Lift up your hearts" and the congregation responds "We lift them up to the Lord!" both celebrant and people could lift their hands upward and outward in a simple gesture.

Consider making use of sung psalm responses, traditional spirituals, and simple chants such as those developed in the Taizé community. These have the quality of musical meditations and foster a reflective capacity in the congregation.

Experiencing Worship When Leading Worship

One of the most difficult aspects of leading worship is that attention to process and logistics can interfere with the ability to experience worship yourself. There is a freedom to receive and participate in the pew that worship leaders rarely share. This does not mean, however, that it is impossible to worship God while leading worship.

How can church professionals find spiritual nourishment in leading worship? The keys to meaningful worship for worship leaders are essentially the same as those already suggested. The place to begin is with adequate preparation.

If you participate in a weekly lectionary study group, you will bring a wealth of fresh insight to the scripture that is read and preached Sunday morning, even if you are the reader and preacher! You will experience a different level of connection to people in the pew who shared their questions and insights with you.

Personal prayer during the week is even more critical for church leaders than for other Christians. Without it, you are truly courting the sin of works-righteousness, not to mention hypocrisy and burnout. Meditate with scripture, listen deeply to God's Word, finding the links between it and your own life before formulating a sermon. This process will change your experience of preaching. You will discover grace in it for yourself as well as for others.

Self-examination before common worship, especially before celebrating the sacraments, is also essential for church leaders. Honest life assessment and confession is a means of grace that is as necessary to pastors and priests as to other Christians. It paves the way to forgiveness and restoration, freeing you to worship God in joy and gratitude. Self-examination allows leaders to acknowledge dependence on divine grace for all effective ministry. It can help worship leaders to relax and let the Spirit work in unplanned ways.

In one church I know of, each Sunday the pastor asked one of his elders to pray for him during the service. The elder went apart to a small room to be given entirely to prayer for the minister during this time. The results were remarkable in the worship experience of both congregation and pastor. Preaching started to "come alive" and the sense of spiritual vitality in the congregation was palpably different. Why not ask faithful lay leaders in your church to pray for you and other worship leaders during the service? They would not necessarily need to leave the sanctuary to do so.

If you are sufficiently prepared for the service in advance, you should be able to participate in worship. Take time to become aware of God's presence and sustaining grace before starting to lead worship. Keep the remembrance of God's real presence before you during the service. Cultivate this awareness, perhaps using a prayer of the heart from time to time: "Be still and know that I am God." "Worship the Lord in the beauty of holiness." "My God and my all." Let go of thoughts about how to phrase that announcement, or whether you can rework a sermon illustration before the Gospel reading. Trust the Spirit to guide and direct your thoughts, words, and affections as you speak. Then you can relax and take in what is going on, even while you guide it. Enter into hymns with your whole heart and receive the anthem as a blessing. Give your attention to the meaning of what you speak. Let everything be an offering to the Holy One in your midst.

Afterward, reflect on how you experienced worship. At what points in the service were you able to be present to God and when did you become distracted or self-absorbed? If you ponder this each week, perhaps making journal entries to help you see your patterns of attitude and attention, you will gradually be able to bring more and more of the Sunday service into your actual experience of worship. Indeed, your awareness of God's presence as the source and center of worship may have a direct impact on how you design and lead the service. You will come to know more truly the difference between performing before a congregation and leading a congregation in common worship before God. We are all actors in the great drama where God is our audience!

Notes

1. Timothy Ware, *The Orthodox Church* (Baltimore: Penguin Books, 1963), 272.
2. Richard J. Foster, *Celebration of Discipline* (San Francisco: Harper & Row, 1988), 159.
3. Walter Wink, "Waging Spiritual Warfare with the Powers," *Weavings* 5, no. 2 (March–April 1990): 34–35.
4. In his book *Into the Light: A Simple Way to Pray with the Sick and Dying* (Nashville: The Upper Room, 1988), Ron DelBene has some excellent, practical suggestions about ways of calling forth the gifts of shut-ins and giving them a sense of community with one another as well as with the congregation.
5. Walter Brueggemann, *Journal for Preachers* 10, no. 2 (Lent 1987): 19.

5 The Practice of Self-Emptying
Rediscovering the Fast

[God] humbled you by letting you hunger, then by feeding you with manna, with which neither you nor your ancestors were acquainted, in order to make you understand that one does not live by bread alone, but by every word that comes from the mouth of the LORD.

Deuteronomy 8:3

Fasting may seem a peculiar discipline to commend to contemporary Christians. It is vaguely repellent to our modern sensibilities. If images of ascetic abuse linger in our historical memory, we may have shoved fasting into that mental closet with hair shirts, chastity belts, and flagellation whips. Why, we wonder, should we turn back to a pinched, life-denying spirituality that glories in restricting the body? Why not glorify God by enjoying the blessings of creation?

What are your general reactions to the idea of fasting? Identify your feelings and reservations below before you read this chapter. Then comment again when you've finished the chapter.

Some of us, no doubt, would be relieved to see the long-revered tradition of fasting fade into oblivion. Yet fasting has been a significant spiritual practice in virtually every religion, and there is good reason to take a fresh look at its purpose and power. The practical rationales for fasting that our culture still accepts, such as health benefits or political clout, do not express the deeper spiritual significance of a fast. I believe we need to recover the spiritual purpose of fasting precisely because of the character of contemporary culture.

In ancient Jewish tradition, fasting had two primary purposes. The first was to express personal or national repentance for sin; fasting was a form of humble supplication before God in the face of imminent destruction or calamity (see Joel 2, Jonah 3, and Esther 4). The second purpose of a fast was to prepare oneself inwardly for receiving the necessary strength and grace to complete a mission of faithful service in God's name. Primary examples are the forty-day wilderness fasts of Moses, Elijah, and Jesus (Exodus 24 and 34, 1 Kings 19, and Matthew 4). The fast prepares each one to become a personal bearer of God's saving acts to the people.

Take a few minutes to stop and reflect: How do you think prayer and fasting might be connected?

Jesus combined prayer and fasting to overcome his temptations in the desert. The early church followed this practice at critical points in its life to discern how God was leading them and to empower their ministry (Acts 13, 14). Some ancient manuscripts indicate that Jesus' cure of an epileptic boy (Mark 9:14–29) was possible only "by prayer and fasting." These examples suggest that the combination of prayer and fasting invites a greater measure of God's power to be released through us than might be possible through prayer alone.

In Jesus' time, regular fasting was a normal part of Jewish piety (Luke 18:12; Matt. 6:16). Its practice was viewed as normal in the life of Christians until quite recently, and it is still seriously practiced by the Eastern Orthodox and Roman Catholic churches. Protestants, however, largely seem to have forgotten that their greatest leaders—figures like Luther, Calvin, Wesley, and Edwards—were strong advocates of this discipline. Wesley prescribed regular fasting on Wednesdays and Fridays. Calvin commended it to (1) subdue the needless desires of "the flesh"; (2) prepare for prayer and meditation; and (3) express humility before God in confession.[1]

While Christian history reveals that at times fasting has been taken to unhealthy extremes, other very sane perspectives emerge from the tradition:

> Abba Joseph asked Abba Poemen, "How should one fast?" Abba Poemen said to him, "For my part, I think it better that one should eat every day, but only a little, so as not to be satisfied."[2]

An "ascetical fast" of this kind serves to remind us of our dependence on God. Even with my limited experience of fasting, I am convinced that "rather than weakening us [it] makes us light, concentrated, sober, joyful, pure. One receives food as a real gift of God. One is constantly directed at that inner world which inexplicably becomes a kind of food in its own right."[3]

Some of our suspicions about fasting may simply be a rationale to cover deeper anxieties. In a land where food is so abundant that we can both glorify and trivialize it, we have developed a horror of being without it. Advertisements bombard us with images of food. The underlying message seems to be, "Eat! Food is good, and good for you. You should never be hungry. But if you are, the remedy is no farther than your friendly pizza delivery service!" Like the noise we have become accustomed to, or the frenetic busyness of our schedules, food is taken for granted as a constant in our lives. The very idea of intentionally being without it for even a day may threaten some of the unconscious assumptions on which our lives are built.

This is precisely why fasting remains so relevant for people of faith today. In a more tangible, visceral way than any other spiritual discipline, fasting reveals our excessive attachments and the assumptions that lie behind them. Food is necessary to life, but we have made it more necessary than God. How often have we neglected to remember God's presence when we would never consider neglecting to eat! Fasting brings us face to face with how we put the material world ahead of its spiritual Source.

Jesus tells us that his "bread" is to do the will of the One who sent him (John 4:31–34). He calls himself "the bread of life" (John 6:35). Are we aware of how much sustains our life apart from physical food? Do we have an inner conviction that *Christ* is our life? We will comprehend little of how we are nourished by Christ until we have emptied ourselves of the kinds of sustenance that keep us content to live at life's surface.

Persons well used to fasting as a systematic practice will have a clear and constant sense of their resources in God.

Dallas Willard

A Look at Lent

One of the best ways to explore the meaning and practice of fasting is to examine how Lent has been understood in the church. Lent is the traditional season of prayer and fasting in preparation for the great "Feast of feasts," Easter. Right away we can see that the church year has been characterized by *rhythms* of feasting and fasting. What real significance can Easter have if we do not know the experience of Lent? The joy and delight of a feast is proportional to the deprivation of a fast. Have we lost the art of true feasting through rejection of the fast?

Lent is the great fast of the church year. It is a season that reveals and magnifies our understanding of spiritual discipline. When I was growing up, Protestants knew little of liturgical seasons; their impressions of Lent came mainly from Roman Catholic

71

friends. The impressions consisted largely of restriction, regulation, and penitence. As Protestants began to recover church seasons, many took on the tradition of "giving things up" for Lent—dessert, chocolate, popcorn, chewing gum, or other food frivolities. What we have participated in and witnessed is the trivialization of a very profound discipline.

We trivialize spiritual disciplines when we lose sight of their real purpose. Lent is not a six-week inconvenience in an otherwise abundant year, during which we somehow please God with voluntary if minor suffering. Lent is not a testing ground for the true grit of our will power. It is certainly not a "spiritual" rationale for losing ten pounds before venturing to the beach in a bathing suit. Do you see how easy it is to twist a practice like fasting into a means to accomplish our own ends? The question we need to ask with any spiritual discipline is, What does God want to accomplish in me through this practice?

For the early church, Lent was just the opposite of a dreary season of restriction and self-torture. It was understood as an opportunity to return to normal human life—the life of natural communion with God that was lost to us in the Fall. This perspective is clearly expressed in Eastern Orthodox liturgy and theology:

> In the Orthodox teaching . . . the world was given to [Adam and Eve] by God as "food"—as means of life. . . . In food itself God . . . was the principle of life. Thus to eat, to be alive, to know God and be in communion with Him were one and the same thing. The unfathomable tragedy of Adam is that . . . he ate "apart" from God in order to be independent of Him . . . because he believed that food had life in itself and that he, by partaking of that food, could be like God, i.e., have life in himself.[4]

In Eden, God gave Adam and Eve every fruit of the garden but one. That one fruit, out of a world of variety, indicated a limit to human freedom. Accepting that limit was the single abstinence required by God. It was a way of recognizing that human beings are dependent on God for life. But Adam and Eve allowed themselves to be seduced by the serpent (a figure of God's enemy, Satan). The serpent's question inverts the reality of the situation: "Did God say, 'You shall not eat of *any* tree of the garden'?" (Gen. 3:1, emphasis added). Instead of a prohibition against one fruit, God's warning is presented as a prohibition against all fruit. The temptation, it seems, is to see a single boundary as so restrictive that it negates the good of all other freedoms. Adam and Eve took the bait. Metaphorically, they "broke the fast," transgressing the one limit required of them. In refusing to accept the natural bounds of their creaturehood, they reached for the very place of God. They wanted it all.[5]

The fallen human now lives as if there were no legitimate limits. While we bow temporarily to practical limitations, limits are to be assaulted through the powers of intelligence and technology until they yield to human ingenuity and control. The appetites are given free reign. It is considered a God-given right to use every resource and creature on earth for personal enjoyment or gain. The goal of human life is to acquire more, to experience more, to stimulate every sense to capacity and beyond.

A life that recognizes no limits cannot recognize the sovereignty of God. When created things have become an end in themselves instead of a means of divine grace, they can no longer offer real life. Death and suffering entered into creation because our human forbears could not "keep the fast."

Did you know that *Lent* is derived from a Saxon word meaning "spring?" In the early church, Lent was viewed as a spiritual spring, a time of light and joy in the renewal of the soul's life. It represented a return to the "fast" that Adam and Eve broke: a life in which God was once more center and source, and the material world was again received as a means of communion with God. This return to authentic human life was made possible by the Incarnation.

The early church found the reversal of Adam's sin in Christ. After his Baptism, Jesus began the work of redemption by keeping a forty-day fast in the wilderness. When he became hungry, he refused the lie that life depends on bread alone and reaffirmed that human beings depend in all things on God for life. He said no to the limitless, self-referential power Satan tempted him with. Every temptation—to self-sufficiency, to self-display, to power at the price of integrity—would have placed Jesus at center stage instead of God. Throughout his life Jesus consistently pointed to *God's* authority, power, and will in him, not to his own. Jesus "kept the fast," abstaining not only from food but from the illegitimate exercise of power. He accepted human limits, living within the normal constraints of human life and accepting a human death. Jesus lived out God's deepest intention for human beings in the created order. Through him, we too begin to live as a "new

Frivolous consumption corrupts the soul away from . . . service to God and injures neighbors as well.
Dallas Willard

Ultimately to fast means only one thing: to be hungry—*to go to the limit of that human condition which depends entirely on food and, being hungry, to discover that this dependency is not the whole truth about [us], that hunger itself is first of all a spiritual state and that it is in its last reality* hunger for God.
Alexander Schmemann

creation." The possibility of genuine communion with God in and through creation is restored.

Perhaps we can see, then, that the discipline of fasting has to do with the critical dynamic of *accepting those limits which are life-restoring.* Our culture would seduce us into believing that we can have it all, do it all, and (even more preposterous!) that we deserve it all. Yet in refusing to accept limits on our consumption or activity, we perpetuate a death-dealing dynamic in the world. That is why the discipline of fasting is so profoundly important today.

Food Fasting

Abstaining from food is the original meaning and most basic expression of a fast. It is the core reality from which analogous forms of abstinence derive. If we are to recapture the practice of such fasting as a spiritual discipline, we need to know how to go about it. Ignorance of basic rules can be dangerous, but if we follow a few simple guidelines there is little danger and much to be gained from a fast.

Russian Orthodox theologian Alexander Schmemann reminds us that first we must prepare spiritually before fasting.[6] Depending on the shifting sands of will power only results in frustration and harm. A fast for spiritual purposes must be centered on God and can be so only if we ask God's help. We must recover both a reverence for our bodies as temples of the Holy Spirit and a genuine respect for food as God's gift. Such inner preparation will give us a vision of the spiritual dimension of fasting, and arm us with the weapons we will need when temptations and difficulties arise.

Richard Foster distinguishes between a normal fast, a partial fast, and an absolute fast. The normal fast "involves abstaining from all food, solid or liquid, but not from water." A partial fast involves "a restriction of the diet but not total abstention." And an absolute fast means "abstaining from both food and water."[7]

The first rule of fasting is not to practice it if sick, traveling, or under unusual stress. If you suffer from any debilitating physical condition or illness, consider a fast only under the strict supervision of a physician. Because a fast depletes your normal energy reserves, it is important to reduce your normal activity while fast-

Fasting is not a renunciation of life; it is a means by which new life is released within us.
          James Earl Massey

Fasting is important in Christian experience because it deepens within the whole self a sense of one's dependence upon the strength of God. Fasting is more than an act of abstinence. It is an affirmative act; it is a way of waiting on God; it is an act of surrender.
          James Earl Massey

ing. Activity that increases energy expenditure—such as travel, undue stress, or heavy physical labor—should normally preclude fasting.

Beyond these considerations, if you are a beginner or have not fasted in a long time, start with a partial fast of not more than twenty-four hours, not more than once a week. Restricting your intake to fresh fruit juices is a good way to engage in a partial fast. For many, it is helpful to begin after the evening meal, fasting until the next day's evening meal, so that only two meals are missed. Some prefer to fast from lunch to lunch, on the same principle.

Give your body several weeks to adjust to regular fasting before you introduce any further stages. After four or five weeks, you will be ready to try a normal fast for the same twenty-four hour period. Drink only water, but *plenty* of it.

In the disciplines of abstinence, we abstain to some degree and for some time from the satisfaction of what we generally regard as normal and legitimate desires.

Dallas Willard

After several months of adjusting to a normal fast, you could choose to move on to a thirty-six-hour fast: all three meals in a given day. It is a common mistake to try to "tank up" on extra calories before fasting, and an equally common error to eat a big meal after one. A fast should be broken gently with a light, non-fatty meal, generally of fruits and vegetables. Longer fasts need to be broken even more gradually. Foster offers specific guidelines on the dynamics of a longer fast, but urges that beyond the thirty-six-hour variety, it is best to discern through prayer whether you are called to a fast of several days or more.

There is no reason to push yourself to heroic effort where fasting is concerned. If you feel tempted to do so, take a hard look at your motives. Has fasting become a source of pride in personal achievement? Are you competing with yourself to win a record? Are you trying to score points with God? "More" is not necessarily "better" in this matter. Perhaps you are called just to be faithful to the humble practice of a short fast once a week. Do not underestimate what God can accomplish in you through the consistent offering of such a discipline.

Other Forms of Fasting

In a culture obsessed with consumption, I believe fasting needs to be considered in terms of its inner dynamic: *abstinence*. The concept of abstinence applies to more than alcohol and sex. It needs

St. Augustine once said that God is always trying to give good things to us, but our hands are too full to receive them. If our hands are full, they are full of the things to which we are addicted. And not only our hands, but also our hearts, minds, and attention are clogged with addiction. Our addictions fill up the spaces within us, spaces where grace might flow. . . . [T]he spiritual significance of addiction is not just that we lose freedom through attachment to things, . . . [but] that we try to fulfill our longing for God *through objects of attachment.*

Gerald May

If we feel that any habit or pursuit, harmless in itself, is keeping us from God . . . ; if we find that things which others can do with impunity are for us the occasion of falling, then abstinence is our only course. Abstinence alone can recover for us the real value of what should have been for our help.

William Ralph Inge

to be considered in relation to the whole of our affluent and addictive lifestyle. Our society voraciously consumes just about any and every thing: food, drink, sex, drugs, guns, cars, clothing, energy, gadgets, TV, computers, videos, gossip, fads, ideologies, programs, even work and leisure. Our intimate relationships have often suffered from this consumer mentality: enjoy while useful and stimulating, discard when no longer satisfying. The world of God's gifts has indeed become a world of mere objects to satisfy temporary and restless appetites.

The point of abstinence is not the denial of all enjoyment in life, for, as Baptist minister and author Dallas Willard rightly points out, "We dishonor God as much by fearing and avoiding pleasure as we do by dependence upon it or living for it."[8] The purpose of abstinence is to learn *rightly* to enjoy God's gifts. We need disciplines of abstinence because we have come to relate to food, drink, sex, money, recognition, and many other things in life not as lovely gifts to be enjoyed in moderation and gratitude, but as objects of consumption to fill emotional voids. When what we consume is consuming us, and what we possess is possessing us, the only way back to health and balance is to refrain from using those things that have control over us. "To give up anything that comes between ourselves and God"[9] is the core dynamic of self-denial.

What forms might this kind of "fasting" take in our lives? One possibility is to abstain from constant media stimulation. Choosing natural sounds or silence over incessant television or radio would be a pertinent form of fasting for many. What about abstaining from eating overpackaged, overprocessed foods? Or from throwing away all packaging in our disposable culture? The recycling movement is only beginning to affect our mountains of needless waste. If your mailbox is like mine, it frequently groans under the weight of mail-order catalogs. I can envision scores of "mail-order junkies," wading daily through this glut of slick advertising, who need to rest their credit cards and reclaim some precious time. Could we fast from needless shopping sprees?

We need to consider abstaining not only from lack of all physical exercise but also from fitness mania; to think of fasting not only from compulsive eating but from compulsive dieting.[10] We have a tendency to fall off the path of moderation into extremes. We like to impress ourselves and others with "the big splash." It is a more difficult discipline to slowly change your eating habits and lose two pounds a week than to lose fifteen pounds quickly and swing back to former eating patterns. Part of fasting in this case is to relinquish the temporary excitement that comes with spectacular achievement. A counterweight to the desire for congratulation is abstaining from personal recognition. We can scarcely make a big splash if we practice anonymity in our charity or engage in our vocation without seeking to be honored.

What would it mean to fast from judging others, or even from judging ourselves too harshly? Most of us are quick to prejudge people we barely know on the basis of external appearance, mannerisms, or a few statements taken out of context. Worse yet, we judge people on hearsay. Spiritually speaking, this is a dangerous habit. Often we are ashamed of our prejudgments (prejudices) when we actually get to know the person in question. To abstain from judging others in the secret places of our heart is a challenging discipline to learn and sustain.

Perhaps one of the most difficult forms of abstaining today is from overpacked schedules, both for ourselves and our children. When we become exhausted, depressed, and short-tempered, when we have little energy left for our friends or families, much less for ourselves, do we give more glory to God?

Do you tend to say yes to too many things? Take some time to examine your motives for doing so. Is there something you are trying to prove? Someone you are trying to save, or to impress? Is it God's will or yours you are following?

With so many ways to practice fasting through abstinence, we clearly need to make choices appropriate to our character and life circumstances. Behind every fitting choice of abstinence lies the question, What do I do to excess? What I do to excess reveals my inordinate desires, my compulsions, the attachments that have control over me. They are precisely the areas of my life that need the freeing lordship of Christ rather than my own abysmally ineffective efforts at control. Fasting is not primarily a discipline through which *I* gain greater control over my life, but one through which *God* gains access to redirect and heal me in body, mind, and spirit.

Review the various forms of fasting suggested in this section. Each one is a way of allowing the Spirit to bring your life under control. Select one in which you need to establish boundaries. Try it for a day. Then commit to a full week. Assess your experience in writing, or talk it through with a Christian friend.

Invitations to Explore

Keeping a Journal during a Fast

If the purpose of your fast is spiritual, your inner attitudes will be of greater significance than your physical reactions. Keeping a journal can help you focus on the spiritual dimensions of a fast. Answering some questions may help your journal-keeping

Fasting makes me vulnerable and reminds me of my frailty. It leads me to remember that if I am not fed I will die. . . . Standing before God hungry, I suddenly know who I am. I am one who is poor, called to be rich in a way that the world does not understand. I am one who is empty, called to be filled with the fullness of God. I am one who is hungry, called to taste all the goodness that can be mine in Christ.

Macrina Wiederkehr

process: How do I respond to hunger pangs? What feelings attend the experience of physical emptiness—panic, irritation, boredom, helplessness? How do I express these? Do I sense any inward cleansing, release, or freedom? Do I feel a need to draw the attention of others to what I am doing? Do I find myself attentive to God's presence in new ways? connected to others in new ways? What is God revealing to me through my responses?

The following excerpts are taken from the journal of a person who, as a spiritual discipline, committed himself to fast once a week for two years. It reveals the kind of growth that can occur through an extended practice of fasting for the sake of God. It is also a good example of the way a journal can be used to help record the movements of the mind and heart.

> I felt it a great accomplishment to go a whole day without food. Congratulated myself on the fact that I found it so easy. Also, enjoyed the fact that I lost weight . . .

> Began to see that the above was hardly the goal of fasting. Was helped in this by beginning to feel hunger . . .

> Began to relate the food fast to other areas of my life where I was more compulsive. . . . to move out of the grip of necessity . . . I did not have to have a seat on the bus to be contented, or to be cool in the summer and warm when it was cold.

> Continued to feel less at the mercy of my own desires—more detached. . . . Reflected more on Christ's suffering and the suffering of those who are hungry and have hungry babies . . .

> Six months after beginning the fast discipline, I began to see why a two-year period had been suggested. The experience changes along the way. Hunger on fast days became acute, and the temptation to eat stronger. For the first time I was using the day to find God's will for my life. Began to think about what it meant to surrender one's life.

> I now know that prayer and fasting must be intricately bound together. There is no other way, and yet that way is not yet combined in me.[11]

Recovering the Fast of Repentance

I have said little thus far concerning the role of fasting as an expression of repentance. Since fasting and repentance are so clearly joined in the Bible, recovering this dimension of a fast seems appropriate and important. John Calvin followed the biblical tradition of interpreting major disasters as divine messages. He urged that when war, famine, plague, or other natural calamities threaten a nation, "the whole people ought to accuse themselves and confess their guilt." He felt that regional threats obligated local pastors "to urge the church to fasting, in order that by supplication the Lord's wrath may be averted."[12] While Calvin's language may seem quaint, the impulse behind it may strike us as rather pertinent.

If ever there was a time when repentance was called for on a national and international scale, it is now. Personal and social sin abounds everywhere we look. World powers stand by while despots wreak havoc on their own populations. Ancient hatreds continue to fuel wars all over the globe. Racial and ethnic tensions threaten the cohesion of our own communities. Levels of violence and addiction exceed all bounds. Family structures crumble, and children become both victims and perpetrators of abuse in their homes and schools. Our way of life places intolerable burdens on the resources of the earth, fouling the very elements we depend on for life.

Even a fraction of this woeful catalog should be enough to put us on our knees! Would not a time of corporate mourning and repentance be in order? Surely our religious leaders could gather and appoint a time of fasting and prayer for all believers. Yet if our leaders will not be so bold, we can take up the invitation to make sincere repentance a key in our personal fasting, and we can intercede on behalf of those who apparently see no need for a change of heart.

Springtime for the Soul

Perhaps we can now see how abstaining from food is connected to other forms of abstinence. Regular fasting at its most basic level may well be the most effective way to deal with all the appetites and compulsions that rule us. Why else would fasting be so heartily recommended by so many saints over so many years? Combined with prayer, it is a potent means of making ourselves available to the cleansing, restoring, empowering grace of God.

Fasting teaches temperance or self-control and therefore teaches moderation and restraint with regard to all our fundamental drives.
Dallas Willard

Abstinence, of course, is not the sum total of the Christian life. It simply creates enough space in us so that the Spirit can creatively use our talents and energies in the service of the Kingdom: "A proper abstinence actually breaks the hold of improper engagements so that the soul can be properly engaged by God."[13] Disciplines of *engagement* balance our practice of abstinence.

Most of the practices considered in this book are disciplines that call us to actively invite God's presence and engage God's purpose in deeper ways: worship, spiritual reading, prayer, self-examination, guidance, and hospitality. Yet coloring and enlivening their practice are aspects of abstinence: silence, solitude, secrecy, and sacrifice. The abstinence of fasting is integrally connected to the engagements of prayer and active service. Indeed, fasting from physical food can scarcely be experienced as spiritual until it is joined to the sense of feasting on God's gracious love and responding by loving others. Fasting prepares us for authentic service. Author Macrina Wiederkehr expresses this connection beautifully:

> Fasting is cleansing. It cleans out our bodies. It lays bare our souls. It leads us into the arms of that One for whom we hunger. In the Divine Arms we become less demanding and more like the One who holds us. Then we experience new hungers. We hunger and thirst for justice, for goodness and holiness. We hunger for what is right. We hunger to be saints.
>
> Most of us are not nearly hungry enough for the things that really matter. That's why it is so good for us to feel a gnawing in our guts. Then we remember why we are fasting. We remember all the peoples of the world who have no choice but to go to bed hungry. We remember how we waste and squander the goods of this world. We remember what poor stewards of the earth we have been. We remember that each of us is called to be bread for the world. Our lives are meant to nourish. Fasting can lead us to the core of our being and make us more nourishing for others.[14]

All forms of spiritual discipline help us to make more space for God in our lives. Fasting and prayer, the traditional disciplines of Lent, seem to be two of the most effective tools in clearing away our self-preoccupation so we can be more responsive to God's life in and through and around us. Perhaps we can think of it this way: fasting is a form of interior "spring cleaning." It involves real labor, but how satisfying and freeing it is to get rid of all that unnecessary stuff!

There is, finally, a light and joyful quality to the practice of fasting. Release, clarity, and freedom shine through the sometimes painful and often tedious process of stripping away what is false in us. Spiritually, the result is restoration to what the Orthodox call "the natural life," which is nothing other than the Christ life: "it is no longer I who live, but it is Christ who lives in me" (Gal. 2:20). May we come to discover more fully in our own experience this springtime of the soul.

Notes

1. John Calvin, *Institutes of the Christian Religion,* ed. John T. McNeill, trans. Ford Lewis Battles (Philadelphia: Westminster Press, 1960), 4. 12. 20, p. 1242.
2. Benedicta Ward, ed., *The Sayings of the Desert Fathers* (Kalamazoo, Mich.: Cistercian Publications, 1975), 144.
3. Alexander Schmemann, *Great Lent* (Crestwood, N.Y.: St. Vladimir's Seminary Press, 1974), 98.
4. Ibid., 94–95.
5. In this interpretation, I am indebted to insights from Alexander Schmemann's *For the Life of the World* (Crestwood, N.Y.: St. Vladimir's Seminary Press, 1973), and to one of his foremost Protestant interpreters, Dr. V. Bruce Rigdon.
6. Schmemann, *Great Lent*, 97.
7. See Richard J. Foster's chapter on fasting in *Celebration of Discipline* (San Francisco: Harper & Row, 1988), 49.
8. Dallas Willard, *The Spirit of the Disciplines* (San Francisco: Harper & Row, 1988), 180.
9. W. R. Inge, *Goodness and Truth* (London: Mowbray, 1958), 76–77.
10. Eating disorders like anorexia and bulimia are true physiological addictions and cannot simply be turned off at will. They require either professional help or a communal therapeutic structure such as a Twelve-Step Program. The language of fasting can be used both to cover and to reinforce eating compulsions.
11. From Elizabeth O'Connor's *Search for Silence* (Waco, Tex.: Word Books, 1971), 103–4. Used by permission of author.
12. Calvin, *Institutes* 4. 12. 15–17, pp. 1242–43.
13. Willard, *The Spirit of the Disciplines*, 176.
14. Macrina Wiederkehr, *A Tree Full of Angels: Seeing the Holy in the Ordinary* (HarperSanFrancisco, 1991), 37.

6   Of Conscience and Consciousness
Self-Examination, Confession, and Awareness

Search me, O God, and know my heart;
test me and know my thoughts.
See if there is any wicked way in me,
and lead me in the way everlasting.
Psalm 139:23–24

Psalm 139 is a beautiful expression of a profound truth: God is the searcher of every human heart, the One from whom no secrets are hidden. God examines and knows every aspect of our being in more intimate detail than we ourselves can see. This may inspire more than a few beads of sweat, or it may give us great comfort. Who is to say whether the verses that follow express an assurance of complete security in God's presence or the near panic of finding no escape from an omnipresent deity?

You hem me in, behind and before,
and lay your hand upon me. . . .
Where can I go from your spirit?
Or where can I flee from your presence?
(Ps. 139:5, 7)

While the truth that we cannot escape God's all-seeing eye may weigh us down at times, it is finally the only remedy for our uneasiness. If we wish to hide from the penetrating gaze of holy love, it is because we know it falls on what is unholy and unloving within us. Only under God's steady gaze of love are we able to find the healing and restoration we so desperately need. When we feel "searched and known" by a gracious God, we are both moved and enabled to search our own hearts honestly. That is why scripture and Christian teaching urge us to examine

Examination of the world without is never as personally painful as examination of the world within. . . . Yet when one is dedicated to the truth this pain seems relatively unimportant.

M. Scott Peck

ourselves and to confess what we find before God and to others. Self-examination and confession do not call us to self-hatred or self-condemnation; they open the door of our heart to cleansing, renewal, and peace.

Points of Departure

We need to know two basic truths if we wish to engage in self-examination as a healthy spiritual discipline. If we do not know these truths in an experiential way, self-examination will be either a superficial exercise or an invitation to despair.

The first truth is the most basic affirmation of our faith: *God loves us.* This is not a general rule to which you, personally, may be an exception. It is not a conditional rule that applies only when you are good, pure, and lovable. God's passionate and personal love for each and every human being expresses who God is. Unfailing love is the divine nature and the divine choice in relation to us. God loves us with an overwhelming love that none of our sins can erase. While we can grieve and disappoint this love, nothing we do or fail to do can alter its depth or reality. It is a gift, a given. We cannot control whether God loves us by efforts to gain this love or even to lose it. Since we neither deserve nor earn such love, God's fondest dream is that we will *receive* and *respond* to it.

Spend some time pondering these two basic truths. Do you find them easy or hard to accept? Why? If you find one easy to believe and the other hard, take a closer look at where your feelings are coming from.

The second truth is our human weakness and brokenness in relation to God. We are creatures damaged by the disorientation of sin. Sin means being "off target," like an arrow wrongly directed. Instead of being aimed toward God, we are aimed toward a distorted image of self. We are directed by self-centered desires, chained to unmet needs, compelled by illusions about who we are and what makes us acceptable or important. We strive to be in control of our lives. In the process, we manipulate those who seem to get in the way, as well as those who appear to be stepping stones to our goals. Our state of misdirection makes us blind. Even if we think we believe in God, we effectively stand in God's place. As long as we are turned in on ourselves, we deny our essential dependence on God. We do not see how compulsively we try to manufacture our own security and meaning in life.

An important turning point in our spiritual life comes when we acknowledge both truths and admit that we can neither earn God's love nor achieve our own security and perfection. We cannot "fix" ourselves or anyone else the way we want to. When we realize that grace lies at the center of life, we start to see in a new way. Turning to face God instead of self is the beginning of Good News, the beginning of personal and relational transformation. Scripture calls this turning "repentance." Facing toward God's tenaciously faithful love frees us to start being real. In the light of God's grace and mercy, we find the courage to look honestly at who we are. Bathed in God's love, we can see clearly and nondefensively all the destructive patterns of our false self: the facades we have hidden behind, the excuses we have relied on to avoid taking responsibility, our habits of deception and control, our failure to love God, others, or ourselves adequately.

The epistle of James instructs the early Christian community, "confess your sins to one another, and pray for one another, so that you may be healed" (5:16). Confession unlocks a process of spiritual healing, opening us to forgiveness, cleansing, reconciliation, and renewal. But we cannot confess our sins unless we know what they are. This is where the art of self-examination comes into play.

Two basic forms of self-examination are described in this chapter. The first, "examination of conscience," is an explicitly penitential practice that helps us name and acknowledge our weaknesses. The second, "examination of consciousness," sharpens our awareness of both positive and negative aspects of our attitudes and behaviors. While related, each practice suggests a somewhat different focus and approach. Both can be daily disciplines, although examination of consciousness is probably easier to practice daily whereas examination of conscience is often recommended as a weekly preparation for common worship.

I want to be perfectly clear that self-examination is not an invitation to psychoanalysis, problem solving, self-lecturing, or ego-absorption. The whole point of self-examination is to become more *God-centered* by observing the moments when we are or are not so.

Empty thy mind of all other cares and thoughts, that they may not distract or divide thy mind. . . . Then fall down before God in hearty prayer, desiring the assistance of his Spirit, to discover to thee the plain truth of thy condition.

Richard Baxter

Examination of Conscience

An examination of conscience is a time when "a soul comes under the gaze of God and . . . is pierced to the quick and becomes conscious of the things that must be forgiven and put right before it can continue to love One whose care has been so constant."[1] In the history of the church, this form of self-examination has been considered an especially significant way to prepare for receiving the sacrament of Communion.

For those who are new to examination of conscience, it is helpful to begin with a "life review." This is an opportunity to look back through your life with a clear and impartial eye. The idea is to observe yourself as if from outside, objectively noting character traits, habits, attitudes, and tendencies across the years. Every effort should be made to put on neither the rose-colored glasses of naive optimism nor the gray-colored glasses of needless pessimism. There is no need to justify, explain, blame, judge, or excuse. You are simply observing yourself with as much detachment as you are capable of by God's grace. Of course you will not achieve perfect impartiality. This is just a beginning in honest self-assessment.

A process of this sort has been commended through many centuries of Christian practice. Not accidentally, it corresponds to the fourth step of the popular Twelve-Step recovery programs. Twelve-Step groups are among the few communities today that take seriously the need for rigorous and specific confession to God and to one another. They perceive real confession to be the ground for authentic reconciliation and transformed living patterns. While this understanding is rooted in biblical faith, many of our churches have abandoned serious confession, imagining that it reflects or reinforces a lack of self-esteem. Certainly people with low self-esteem can use confession to express feelings of lack of worth, but this is not the purpose of confession. It is precisely because we are worth so much in God's eyes, and ought so to value one another and ourselves, that we confess our shortcomings. We place our hope in God's forgiveness and renewal, trusting that changeable attitudes and behaviors do not indelibly define who we are. A true spirit of confession actually increases authentic self-acceptance and love.

Step four of a Twelve-Step program is to "make a fearless and searching moral inventory of ourselves." A "fearless inventory" will identify those personality traits, inclinations, attitudes, and behaviors that interfere with our truest good and the good of others (i.e., with God's will). We discover where and why our lives and relationships are out of order. The immediate effect of such rigorous truthfulness is self-knowledge. The larger purpose is to sur-

Self-examination is not morbid introspection or self-condemnation, but the honest, fearless confrontation of the self, and its abandonment to God in trust.

Kenneth Leech

render our destructive, maladaptive life patterns to God so that we can become more fully the person God intends. This "step" offers a practical and concrete model for a life review.[2]

Before starting, several points need clarification. First, a process like this may take many days or even weeks to complete. You will discover very little about yourself if you try to rush it.

Second, you can be sure that shining the light of truth into places until now left uninspected will elicit uncomfortable emotions like fear, guilt, shame, and embarrassment. It is important to acknowledge these feelings and let them be real. At the same time, these feelings should not be allowed to control you or prevent self-examination.

Third, assume that you will not see all your character flaws right away. The self-protection of denial will be at work. You need to let go of the perfectionism by which you imagine you can figure out and fix yourself by your own sheer astuteness. In self-examination, we rely on the grace of God to give us insight into who we are and how we behave. God knows what we are ready to look at and when we need to do so.

Finally, you need to resist the temptation to focus attention on what others have done to you in the past. What others have done to you is their responsibility, not yours. Self-examination is an opportunity to discover the problematic parts of your own attitudes and choices.

The following process describes one way to do a life review.[3] The full benefit of this review comes with undertaking the process twice: once to identify personal weaknesses (the basic focus in examination of *conscience*), and once to identify personal strengths and learnings. Linked together, these two phases of the life review correspond well with the examination of *consciousness*. Because the first phase provides an excellent foundation for daily examination of conscience, I will focus primarily on the confessional phase of the life review in this section.

Life Review

Take several pieces of paper and write a single focus at the top of each, such as Fears, Resentments, Emotional Security, Material Security, Social Acceptance, Sexuality, and Faith. While there is a certain logic to the order as listed, you may treat the topics in any order you choose. Taking each theme in turn, go back to your earliest memories and gradually move forward in time. For example, identify your particular fears and resentments (people, circumstances, institutions) from childhood through the present. Write them down. For each one, identify the effects and how you contributed to the problem. Use "I language," so that you describe your own feelings and experiences rather than blaming others. The following example of a resentment is offered to help you see the process more clearly. I have chosen a childhood experience because gaining greater understanding of experiences from the past can often help us see more clearly the behavior and attitude patterns in our adult life.

Resentment: I am resentful of my elementary school classmates.

Cause: I did not feel accepted socially when I entered fourth grade as a new student. I felt excluded from conversation and games because I was different.

Effects: Hurt, withdrawal, loss of confidence, defensiveness, resentment, pattern of hiding real feelings, nursing pride, determination to prove myself, fear of rejection, self-pity.

My Contribution: I didn't take any initiative to make friends, expected others to move first, and generally allowed myself to be "victimized."

When you look at your character weaknesses in relation to emotional and material security, a somewhat altered process may help. List by name the persons with whom you have recurring problems, or who have deeply affected your sense of physical and emotional security. Note the feelings that attend each relationship, and the cause of those feelings in your experience. But instead of naming the cause in terms of "what she or he did to me," name your basic needs or desires that were not met, or the boundaries that were transgressed. Then consider the effects in your life. For example:

Person: My spouse

Feelings: Pain, shame, anger, depression, confusion

Cause: Loss of self-respect, not feeling accepted, loss of love

Effects: Tend to accept as true what others say about me; don't trust my own perceptions; feel helpless even when I could do something; sometimes take out my frustration on the kids

When you examine events or experiences that have affected your sense of material security, include financial issues. What are your attitudes toward money, and where do they come from? How do they affect your way of life now? Look at your way of relating to food, drink, clothing, and other material goods.

When you examine your sexuality, list specific behaviors and the attitudes that lie behind your actions. Include the effects in your life and the ways your behavior has affected others. With issues of social acceptance, consider the relationships you have had that were painful or unsatisfying. How are these experiences related to a desire for attractiveness, status, recognition, or achievement? What reactions do you typically have to painful social situations? Do you harm others by your response?

An important part of a life review concerns your experiences and struggles in faith. Who is God for you? What is your God-image and how did it develop? Is your current image of God the same image you had as a child? Have you tried to manipulate or use God for your own agenda? What kind of relationship have you had with the church? Have you ever tried to use spiritual practices (prayer, Bible study, service) to make yourself perfect or to "fix" others? What feelings accompany these efforts? What are the effects on you and on others?

Remember that while the first phase of a life review is basically confessional, the process is not complete until you have taken time to observe your gifts and acknowledge your strengths as well. So when you have finished this inventory, go back through each category and ask what personal strengths you brought to the circumstances and relationships you identified. What positive character traits and attitudes have developed out of your life experience? What did you learn in each situation? List these in writing. Often negative traits are the reverse side of a positive trait you have not fully recognized or developed. It is important to realize that grace has been and continues to be at work in you even through the problematic parts of your life.

You may find yourself confessing to God and seeking grace at many points in this process. However, once you have completed the entire review, you are ready to "confess your life" to God in prayer. You can say, in effect, "God, here are the patterns I see at work in my life. This is who I know myself to be, and how I know

The most overlooked feature of genuine humility is the quiet acceptance of our strengths—those qualities God-given which are just as surely ours as our limitations and weaknesses.

Ronald V. Wells

myself to act. Yet you know more than I do. Bring me to greater clarity and understanding of myself. Let every true need in me be filled by you, every wound and defective response be healed and taken into your will. And thank you for these particular gifts and learnings that are part of my life journey. Strengthen them in me and help me share them with others."

The entire process of a life review is generally done only once. The first phase of that process gives us an opportunity to identify the flaws of character, attitude, belief, and response that typically permeate our personal history. Becoming aware of these faults and their underlying causes puts us in a better position to keep an observant eye on ourselves through daily self-examination. I am speaking of self-examination now in its confessional sense (examination of conscience).

Daily Self-Examination

There are several ways to go about a daily practice of self-examination. For example, the Twelve-Step program calls for a "daily inventory," in which you try to identify particular instances of general character weaknesses discovered in life review. A specific list helps you examine your behavior; it might include traits such as selfishness, dishonesty, resentment, fear, jealousy, self-pity, greed, envy, and hatred. You are free to leave off whatever does not apply to you and to add traits that do. Pride, lust, impatience, procrastination, irresponsibility, judgmentalism, and lack of faith could be added. No doubt you will find your own relevant categories. An important part of this step is to name specific ways these faults surfaced in your behavior today, and to indicate how you will make amends to anyone who might have been hurt by them.

Try this exercise on two consecutive days. Reflect on your behaviors and attitudes in light of the Ten Commandments (Exod. 20:1–17) the first day. Do the same with the Beatitudes (Matt. 5:1–11) the next day. Does one approach help you to see yourself more clearly than the other? Why? Does one move you to a greater desire for holy living? Why?

There are other patterns for self-examination and confession in our Christian heritage. Historically, Eastern Orthodox Christians have used the Beatitudes as a liturgical aid to confession, while the Ten Commandments have more typically served that function in Roman Catholic tradition. Protestants have used both.[4] The classic pattern of "Examen of Conscience" in the Roman Catholic monastic tradition involves five steps: gratitude for graces given, prayer for the light of insight, particular and general self-examination, acts of sorrow and contrition, and the resolution to do better.

There is a balance in Christian tradition between private and corporate confession. The Puritans, who felt liberated from priestly confessionals, often used their private diaries to record highly introspective self-examinations before God. The intensely personal nature of these written disclosures was the primary reason so many journals were burned upon the author's death. Yet Puritans joined every major branch of the church in stressing the necessity of common confession in public worship.

Meeting with a Fellow Pilgrim

There is also a kind of middle ground between purely private and purely corporate forms of confession. It is the age-old tradition of confessing to one particular brother or sister in faith. Before the rise of the professional priesthood, Christians confessed to each other and prayed for each others' healing. In the desert tradition of the fourth to the sixth centuries, it was accepted practice to seek out a spiritually mature person—an "elder," or in more personal terms, a spiritual father or mother—who was more often than not a lay monk or hermit.[5] People unburdened their hearts to the elders in confession and sought from them assurance of God's forgiveness. Over time the practice of confession became formalized in church liturgy, and the role of confessor became identified with the ordained priesthood. But alongside such official confession the less formal practice of meeting with a trusted friend or elder continued through the centuries. We can still seek out holy hearts among the people of God to listen to our deepest hurts and hopes.

Author Richard Foster describes a moving incident in his own life when he chose to meet with a trusted and faithful friend for this purpose.[6] He had sensed that something in his past was impeding the flow of God's grace and power in his ministry. So he divided his life into three periods: childhood, adolescence, and adulthood. On three consecutive days, he examined one of these periods before the gaze of God, asking the Lord to reveal to him anything that needed healing or forgiveness. In a state of silent prayer and meditation, he wrote down everything that surfaced in his memory, without analyzing or judging it. Then he went to his chosen friend-confessor, and read what he had written. His friend heard in silence, took the paper and shredded it

Have you ever confessed to a faithful friend? If so, what was this experience like? If not, can you think of anyone to whom you would be drawn to share a confession?

91

into a waste basket, offered a brief word of absolution, then prayed for the healing of every hurt and sorrow of the past. Foster emerged from that experience with a new freedom. It was a profound turning point in his spiritual journey.

Other circumstances might call for a different process. For example, you may be perfectly aware of a particular sin that is eating away your peace of mind. If it is within your power to confess directly to a person you have wounded, pray for the courage and humility to do so. If you have no way to contact the offended party, seek out a friend in Christ whose faith, compassion, and confidentiality you trust. Perhaps you will simply tell your story and receive your friend's response. If the offense seems too painful to speak of, write it out and let your friend read it. There may be times when you cannot bring yourself to reveal a particularly shaming thought or act. Then you can ask for your friend's assistance: "I need your help. There is a sin that I cannot bring myself to confess."[7] Perhaps the friend can help you find a way to bring into the open whatever is terrorizing that dark corner of your soul. If not, seek out a pastor, priest, or experienced spiritual director for help.

Naturally you will not choose to share deeply personal confessions with someone you do not trust implicitly. Exercise discretion in your selection, and ask if your friend is willing to take on this role.

In some cases you may want the assurance of God's forgiveness through an ordained representative of the church. While I do not mean to deny the power of sacramental absolution from sin in corporate worship or the value of liturgical assurances of pardon, the power of face-to-face interaction can effect tremendous release.

I know one Protestant pastor who, in the absence of a theology that sanctions personal absolution, has created his own ritual. It occurs in the context of pastoral counseling and in the privacy of his study. In this simple rite the person suffering guilt is marked with the sign of the cross on the forehead, reminded of his or her baptism, and assured of God's enduring love.

Don't be afraid to ask your pastor about the possibility of such a rite if your church tradition does not already include one.

Examination of Consciousness

So far, I have been speaking of the more explicitly confessional side of self-examination. But as noted earlier, the art of self-

92

examination has a larger context than confession alone. Since "examination of conscience" has become associated with a penitential purpose, a different phrase has emerged to describe the broader focus of self-examination: "examination of consciousness."[8]

Examination of consciousness is a process of becoming aware of the contents of our consciousness, so that we can respond before God in an appropriate way. It is more concerned with the level of our awareness than with particular character flaws and behavioral lapses. In this practice, we pay attention to both the good and the bad, noticing our state of mind and heart during various events and interactions each day. The purpose is twofold: to see where God's grace has been present in our day, and to see where we have or have not responded to that grace.

What we call "consciousness" includes awareness of both external and internal realities. We are conscious of physical, sensory data: the places, people, events, sights, sounds, tastes, smells, and textures of life. We are also conscious of mental and emotional data: our thoughts, questions, beliefs, commitments, observations, feelings, and suspicions.

Examination of consciousness, then, will naturally include both external and internal data. When we reflect on what happened outwardly, we need to be aware of what was going on internally at the time. We are not automatically aware of our feelings, questions, or beliefs in the midst of a given encounter or event. Sometimes we can't quite articulate a question or conviction floating around inside us. Then when someone gives us the words or framework for understanding our actual questions or beliefs, it seems to be a genuine revelation! We may not know how we really feel about something until well after it happens; perhaps our feelings seemed like something else at the time. Noticing physical clues can help us become more fully aware of our "inner data." The turmoil in my stomach may tell me that I was feeling fear, not just surprise. The tension in my shoulders may indicate that I was angry as well as shocked. Questioning ourselves can help to clarify the nature of our feelings as well: Why was I feeling off balance in that conversation? Is my worry justified, or merely compulsive?

Finally, we are noticing what lies behind our feelings and reactions. What motivated my response? Was it basically fear, pride, or greed (self-preservation)? Was it genuine concern for another, love of creation, desire for God's will (self-giving)? Looking back over the thoughts, events, and interactions of the day, we come to the ultimate question: "Was it your love, God, that moved me?"[9] If we can say yes to that question with a clear conscience, self-examination will lead to gratitude for the grace of staying in touch with our living Source. If our answer is no, we will be led to confess our failure and seek the grace of forgiveness and renewed strength.

Behind this practice of self-examination lies a very basic assumption: we have made a choice to offer ourselves to God's service, and we have an active desire to live in God's presence, being led by the Holy Spirit each day. We examine our minds and hearts in order to see clearly where we have been led, when we have had a sense of God's presence, and where or when we have lost that connection. Questions can guide us: How has God been present to me through the people and situations I have encountered this day? Have I been aware of divine presence? Where have I been responding to the Spirit today? Where have I not responded? Why?

Invitations to Explore

Below you will find two simple processes of self-examination that may prove helpful in your daily spiritual practice. The first, "life-centered prayer," is a modern expression of examination of conscience. The second, "a daily practice with journal writing," is a contemporary form of examination of consciousness.

Life-Centered Prayer

Ben Campbell Johnson speaks of learning to "pray with our lives." He suggests a basic process to "integrate the life of prayer into the ordinary events and decisions of everyday life."[10]

Gather the day. Identify the ten or twelve major events of your day, including prayer, particular conversations, meetings, meals, work, and other activities. List them.

Review the day. Reflect upon each occurrence listed, without judging yourself, avoiding feelings, or making excuses. This is the actual substance of your daily life.

Give thanks for the day. Thank God for each part of your day, for your life, and for God's presence in the midst of it.

Confess your sin. Acknowledge your faults in thought, word, and deed toward God, your neighbor, and yourself (you might add the creation, too).

Seek the meaning of the events. Reflect on the larger significance of each event in your life, asking yourself such questions as, What is God saying to me? What am I being called to do? How is this connected to the rest of my life? Write down what comes to mind.

A Daily Practice with Journal Writing

Author and spiritual director Tilden Edwards has described a basic form of daily examination developed by the Shalem Institute in Bethesda, Maryland. This practice emphasizes contemplative awareness and is not intended to be intense or analytical. It is short—only five to ten minutes: "a light, open glance at the day . . . with a desire for its fragments to be recollected in God."[11] I have adapted the process and suggest that you note down your observations in a journal. Keep these notes short and simple; even incomplete phrases are sufficient to capture the essence of your learnings. While this step adds a few more minutes to the process, it is well worth it for the record it gives you over time.

Begin by relaxing your mind. Gently remind yourself of God's presence, and get in touch with your desire to be attentive to that presence during your day. You might offer a simple prayer that the graces of the day will be revealed to your consciousness.

You need not try to find things; simply be "still and open, listening for what might rise from the day." When something surfaces, pay attention to the nature of the grace involved. How was God present? Let yourself feel and express gratitude for the gift.

Then notice how you were present to God or others in the midst of that moment. If you observe that you were unaware of grace, or unresponsive—perhaps holding the reins of ego control—you might breathe a simple prayer like "Lord, have mercy." Let yourself be aware of desire to respond differently another time.

If you observe that you were conscious of, or at least responsive to grace, simply "smile to God with thanksgiving."

Allow something else from your day to rise into awareness; repeat the process. "Thus you are noticing both the hidden presence of God in the day, and your own way of participating in, missing, or resisting that presence."

When you have completed your observations, make note of any responses that seem significant to you. Have you seen something surprising? discovered a pattern in your way of being present to others? received a special sense of grace or gratitude today?

We can see that this is not necessarily a "confessional" process, although we are willing to look openly at ourselves for whatever may be revealed. When practiced daily, it offers a useful way to observe the movements of our heart over time.

Perhaps no other practices enable us to see so clearly where God's grace is present in the daily round of routine tasks and relationships, or to see how we are responding to grace. Daily self-examination is closely allied to prayer. It is also a natural aid to the ongoing relationship of spiritual guidance I describe in chapter 7.

A True Spirit of Confession

The spirit of confession can be genuine or false. Genuine confession is marked by humility, while the counterfeit is riddled with anxiety and pride. Whenever we become fascinated by our sins or sucked into despair over our weaknesses, we may be sure that false humility is at work.

Teresa of Avila, a magnificent teacher on the subject of humility, warned her nuns:

> Now be also on your guard, daughters, against some types of humility given by the devil in which great disquiet is felt

about the gravity of our sins. This disturbance can afflict in many ways even to the point of making one give up receiving Communion and practicing private prayer. These things are given up because the devil makes one feel unworthy. . . . The situation gets so bad that the soul thinks God has abandoned it because of what it is; it almost doubts [God's] mercy.[12]

Self-absorbed anxiety about sin is called "scrupulosity" in Christian tradition. It leads us to think obsessively about our faults, to wallow in guilt, to punish ourselves mentally. Beneath this self-condemnation lies a form of spiritual pride that gives such weight to our sin we imagine ourselves unredeemable: "I'm so awful even God can't forgive me!" Lack of confidence in God's grace is an expression of pride as well as fear.

The only remedy, Teresa tells us, is to "stop thinking about your misery, insofar as possible, and turn your thoughts to the mercy of God, to how [God] loves us and suffered for us."[13] As soon as we see that our thoughts are revolving endlessly around our own sins, we need to lift our eyes to the One who hung on a cross for those sins. When we can personally receive the love offered there, the focus shifts from sin to grace.

Authentic humility keeps us facing God. It teaches us to accept the fact that we will falter and fail. When we fall into temptation, humility prevents us from vicious self-recrimination and simply turns us back to God's love and help. Clear-eyed humility takes the place of wounded pride. Then the self-consuming flames of shame can become cleansing tears of sorrow, which turn into tears of gratitude before God's healing grace. That is why Teresa can say with full assurance, "Humility does not disturb or disquiet or agitate, however great it may be; it comes with peace, delight, and calm."[14]

Offered in this spirit, there is a certain lightness to self examination. If we find ourselves attuned to grace, we are moved to gratitude for blessings already perceived. If we are out of tune with the Spirit, we seek the blessing of forgiveness, healing, and restored awareness of divine grace. There is no way to lose!

Self-examination is an occasion for spiritual refreshment, whatever we discover within ourselves at the time of review. Its purpose is always to bring us into greater intimacy with the Lover of our souls, so that we can learn to walk according to God's path for us. Indeed, the practice of self-examination will only blossom

Especially take heed, if unregenerate, not to conclude of thy future state by the present. Do not say, "Because I am ungodly, I shall die so; because I am a hypocrite, I shall continue so." Do not despair. Nothing but thy willingness can keep thee from Christ, though thou hast hitherto abused him, and dissembled with him.

Richard Baxter

On our bad days we are affirmed as forgiven sinners; on our good days we are affirmed as blessed children.

Richard J. Hauser

out of a genuine *desire* to belong more completely to God and to love as God loves.

The Fruits of Self-Examination

There are many benefits to daily self-examination. Exercised under the penetrating gaze and guiding grace of the Spirit, it leads to healthy self-awareness. Tradition tells us that knowledge of self and knowledge of God go hand in hand. We only know who we really are in relation to God, and knowledge of God leads us to perceive our true status. Since it belongs to the work of the Spirit to reveal us to ourselves, we are incapable of clear self-knowledge apart from grace. Examination of consciousness is a means to self-awareness in relation to God's love.

A result of increasing self-awareness is increasing truthfulness. Humility allows us to be real. We no longer have to put on a good face or a false front. There is no need to impress or to hide. We are not trying to protect or advance ourselves in God's eyes. Truthfulness gives us the freedom to let go of pretense and start living in simple honesty. This is one expression of Jesus' promise, "you will know the truth, and the truth will make you free" (John 8:32).

One of the most precious results of self-knowledge is greater compassion. The more clearly we see ourselves, the harder it becomes to judge the weaknesses and failures of others. We discover that we continually stumble on the path, even when we fervently desire to grow more Christlike and have committed ourselves to love and serve in his name. Self-examination helps us see the circumstances under which we fall into patterns like jealousy, rationalization, hostility, reactions to insecurity, self-defeating behaviors, and desire for prestige or material wealth. We begin to see through the distorted motives of the human heart and understand from personal experience the attraction of evil.

As we perceive the realities of sin in ourselves, we can identify with the brokenness of others. Instead of condemning someone whose behavior is irritating or unacceptable, we may recall similar behavior in our own lives. This doesn't make the behavior more palatable, but it gives us a different perspective on the wounds of the person behaving under compulsion. We can learn to separate the unworthiness of a person's behavior from the worthiness of that person's being as a child of God. We may

A brother at Scetis committed a fault. A council was called to which Abba Moses was invited, but he refused to go to it. Then the priest sent someone to say to him, "Come, for everyone is waiting for you." So he got up and went. He took a leaking jug, filled it with water and carried it with him. The others came out to meet him and said to him, "What is this, Father?" The old man said to them, "My sins run out behind me, and I do not see them, and today I am coming to judge the errors of another." When they heard that they said no more to the brother but forgave him.

The Sayings of the Desert Fathers

even find ourselves praying for people we never imagined we could pray for!

Self-examination allows us to become people who are at peace with ourselves, and who can therefore make peace with others. Compassion bears fruit in forgiveness. Without a sense of complicity in the common human condition of sin, it would be impossible to forgive others. As we see our weaknesses released and healed by a gracious God, we become capable of sharing the gift with others. God's freely offered love softens our hearts, so that we can free others from the cords of our judgment. Such forgiveness is the ground of reconciliation and the beginning of all peacemaking.

There is much more to discover about the art of self-examination. With practice, examination of consciousness teaches us how to discern the movements of the Spirit in our heart. We begin to see more clearly what is of God and what is not. This art is called "discernment of spirits." It prepares us to make choices and life decisions that accord with God's intentions for us.[15] Guidance from a Christian who is experienced in this art can significantly help our growth in the practice of self-awareness and discernment of spirits. Chapter 7 will lead us into an exploration of the nature of spiritual guidance.

Notes

1. Douglas V. Steere, *On Beginning from Within* (New York: Harper & Brothers, 1943), 80.
2. Keith J. Miller's *A Hunger for Healing Workbook* (San Francisco: HarperSanFrancisco, 1992) is a helpful interpretation of Twelve-Step programs as a model for Christian spiritual growth. I use the basic format of his fourth step process in the section "Life Review."
3. This material is adapted from pp. 49–72 of Keith J. Miller's *A Hunger for Healing Workbook* in the form of a highly condensed paraphrase with my own examples. I am much indebted to Mr. Miller for working out such a useful, concrete process of life review.
4. As recently as 1946, the Presbyterian Book of Common Worship included a "Service of Preparation for Holy Communion" that uses the Beatitudes to help the faithful examine their hearts before receiving the Lord's Supper.

5. The term *monk* originally referred to both men and women. See Parker J. Palmer, "Born Again: The Monastic Way to Church Renewal," *Weavings* 9, no. 1:12.

6. See Richard J. Foster, *Celebration of Discipline: The Path to Spiritual Growth* (San Francisco: Harper & Row, 1988), 149–50.

7. Foster, *Celebration of Discipline*, 154.

8. I make this distinction for clarification. In historical terms, "examination of conscience" has often included awareness of the graced moments of our lives along with our miserable failings. The practice of Examen outlined by Saint Ignatius (sixteenth-century founder of the Jesuit order) included discerning "consolations" and "desolations." Consolation refers to that state in which we experience the presence and grace of God, and it calls for gratitude. Desolation represents the opposite state, and it calls for confession. Richard Baxter, the seventeenth-century English Puritan, also describes how self-examination leads to knowledge of a grace-filled or grace-less state of heart.

9. Tad Dunne, *Spiritual Mentoring* (San Francisco: Harper & Row, 1991), 101. See his chapter 5 for a more complete discussion of the art of noticing what is in us.

10. These quotes and the following paraphrase of process are taken from Ben Campbell Johnson's *Invitation to Pray* (Decatur, Ga.: CTS Press, 1992), 18–22.

11. This quote and all quoted materials in the process that follows are from Tilden Edwards, *Living in the Presence: Disciplines for the Spiritual Heart* (San Francisco: Harper & Row, 1987), 84.

12. *The Collected Works of St. Teresa of Avila*, Vol. II, trans. Kieran Kavanaugh and Otilio Rodriguez (Washington D.C.: Institute of Carmelite Studies, 1980), 189.

13. *The Collected Works of St. Teresa*, 190.

14. Ibid., 189.

15. For further reading on this subject, see William Barry and William Connolly, *The Practice of Spiritual Direction* (New York: Seabury Press, 1982); John English, *Spiritual Freedom* (Guelph, Ontario: Loyola House, 1977); Tadd Dunne, *Spiritual Mentoring* (San Francisco: Harper & Row, 1991).

7 Companions on the Journey
The Gift of Spiritual Direction

Spiritual direction is the act of paying attention to
God, calling attention to God, being attentive to God
in a person or circumstances or situation. . . . It
notices the Invisibilities in and beneath and around
the Visibilities. It listens for the Silences between the
spoken Sounds.

Eugene H. Peterson

I am starting to realize that God is only real to me in my head. I believe
in God, and sometimes I think about God, but I don't know if I've
ever really experienced God. I'm not very aware of God most of the
time. I'd like to be, but I'm not sure how to make it happen. I guess
I'd like to talk to someone who knows God from experience.

My life feels off-center right now. I think I'm spending too much time
working. But I get itchy if I'm not doing something productive. I
know I don't pray enough and sometimes I feel guilty about it. But
my prayers don't seem to get results, so I've pretty much given up.
Maybe I'm not praying right. I wonder if I could find a person with
a real prayer life to talk to.

I'm in transition right now. Everything seems to be changing. All the
things I thought were settled are shifting. I feel that maybe God is asking me to consider something new, but I'm not sure what. I want very
much to know what God's will for me is. This is the question I keep
wrestling with. But I'm pretty confused. I don't know how to "read
the signals" when my life is in so much flux. I'd like to be clear about
what God wants for me. I wish there was someone who could help
me discern God's will.

God has taught me a lot over the years. I know from experience the
power of prayer. Sometimes I've kept a journal that has been tremen-
dously helpful in my spiritual growth. But I'm too sporadic about my
spiritual disciplines, even though I know how fruitful they are. I'd like
to covenant with someone else who's been on the journey, just to
encourage me and make me more accountable.

Do any of these voices echo part of your experience? They are representative of many people in our churches. For different reasons, each expresses a desire to have a companion on the journey of faith—a fellow Christian who can speak to his or her condition. Perhaps that condition is a desire to know the reality of God from personal experience. Perhaps it is the hunger to trust a God who is all too real and frightening. It may simply be a desire to live more faithfully and compassionately in God's world, or a yearning to grow into deeper intimacy with the Lover of human souls.

Have you ever felt a need for a person who could occasionally offer guidance, support, or creative challenge in your faith journey? If so, your desire joins you with unnumbered ranks of Christians across the centuries who have sought "spiritual direction."

Spiritual Direction in the Christian Tradition

Spiritual direction, classically understood, is essentially the relationship of a teacher and learner in the area of practicing the spiritual life. Every faith tradition in the world has teacher-learner relationships. Spiritual teachers have various names: prophets, priests, rabbis, roshis, gurus, elders, mentors. They are generally people who give visible evidence of a certain maturity or level of mastery on a particular spiritual path. Learners also have different names: followers, disciples, novices, apprentices. They are people who are drawn to inner growth, yet often find themselves stumbling or wandering in confusion when they attempt to walk a spiritual path alone.

Jesus, like prophets and rabbis before him, gathered disciples and taught them daily, both publicly and privately. His example is the cornerstone of spiritual guidance in the Christian tradition. It is a deeply personal pattern of relationship. What Jesus taught had significance because of who he was. He embodied what he taught. In its early phases, the relationship with his disciples reflected certain characteristics of a parent-child or master-servant relationship, but without authoritarian qualities. As it progressed, the relationship developed traits of a more mutual friendship (see John 15:12–17; 21:15–17).

The apostle Paul was a strong teacher and mentor to the fledgling churches he established. He called himself a "father through the gospel" to his Corinthian congregation (1 Cor. 4:15) and saw

Every Christian should try to consult some learned person. . . . Those who walk in the way of prayer have the greater need of learning; and the more spiritual they are, the greater is their need.

Teresa of Avila

himself as a mother "in labor" to bring forth Christ in the balky Galatian church (Gal. 4:19). We have noted that between the fourth and sixth centuries, Christians flocked to the deserts of Egypt and Arabia to consult on personal spiritual matters with the elder monks of the desert. These monks firmly established the deep-rooted tradition of "spiritual fathers and mothers" in the church. They offered advice, words of wisdom, parables, personal examples of Christian life, and sometimes simple silence as means of direction. Through the centuries, spiritual direction has been provided by priests, monks, ministers, and elders in the church. Protestants have typically called it "pastoral counsel" or "spiritual consultation" and have often given it in small groups or families rather than individually.

But in Christianity, spiritual guidance is not the sole preserve of those who have a special call or training to carry on the tradition. It can be offered by any layperson who is seen to be mature enough in faith to offer guidance to others. The Christian church trusts that the Holy Spirit is active within the community of believers. The grace of the Spirit is given to all Christians, not only to its ministers and priests. Professed vows and ordination are no guarantee of spiritual maturity! Different graces are given to different people according to God's wisdom. Some lay persons are more gifted in spiritual guidance than many clergy. This has been so since the time of the early church.

Spiritual directors themselves participate in a dimension of childlikeness: they sit with the person, listening and responding to movements of truth that come from beyond their management and possession.

Tilden Edwards

Very few have ever been true "masters" of the Christian spiritual life, and those who come closest would never claim the title. A spiritual guide need only be one who has traveled some distance along the path of the Christian life. A guide should be knowledgeable about the markers that lead forward on this path, as well as familiar with the pitfalls, detours, trials, and temptations along its course. Such a person will reflect something of the character of Christ as a result of following in his way. A Christian who gives no evidence of humility, wisdom, compassion, or the ability to speak truth in love will not likely be sought out as a spiritual guide.

What Does a Spiritual Director Do?

Spiritual direction is basically the guidance one Christian offers another to help that person "grow up in every way...into

Christ" (Eph. 4:15). A spiritual guide is someone who can help us see and name our own experience of God. Each of us needs to grow out of second-hand faith to a knowledge of the way the Spirit works in our own lives. We need to learn to recognize the daily tracings of divine grace and to respond to them. At times, spiritual guides will teach, admonish, or confront us firmly in love to hold us accountable for our attitudes and behaviors. But more often spiritual directors act as companions, encouraging and supporting us, praying for us, listening to us, and sharing the learnings of their own life journeys.

Spiritual guides have certain responsibilities. The list that follows describes what spiritual directors typically do:

1. *A spiritual guide listens to us.* When we need someone to hear our life story in terms of faith, a spiritual guide offers hospitable space for us to speak and be heard. Often we do not fully know our thoughts or experiences, our questions or unresolved issues. We do not know until we have had a chance to put them into words before an attentive and receptive ear. A spiritual director can "listen us into clarity," helping us articulate our thoughts, feelings, questions, and experiences in relation to God.

2. *A spiritual guide helps us to notice things.* God's presence and the ways of the Spirit are not generally self-evident to us. They are subtle and unobtrusive, often hidden in the midst of ordinary events and interactions. It takes practice to see the grace of God in everyday life. A spiritual mentor can help us pay attention to signs of grace, to listen for God's "still, small voice" in our daily encounters and experiences. A guide can also direct our attention to the dynamics of our heart, so that we can become more aware of how God speaks to us through it.

3. *A spiritual guide helps us to respond to God with greater freedom.* When we begin to notice God's presence, guidance, provision, and challenge in our daily lives, we are faced with choices. How shall we respond? The choice is not always easy. God's presence and provision are comforting, naturally eliciting gratitude and praise. But God also faces us with the darker realities in our lives, calling us to genuine change. It is hard to let go of old habits and ways of being. Out of this encounter, God calls us to a new sense of purpose and mis-

So what does the spiritual director teach? In the simplest and also most profound terms, the spiritual director is simultaneously a learner and a teacher of discernment. What is happening? Where is God in this person's life? What is the story? Where does this person's story fit in our common Christian story?
Margaret Guenther

Experiences that occur at the edge of silence, come as an undifferentiated mass of feelings, inspirations and intuitions. Not until I can put these into words do the experiences become understandable to me.
Ben Campbell Johnson

104

sion in life. A spiritual director can encourage us toward a fuller freedom to respond to God in loving obedience.

4. *A spiritual guide points us to practical disciplines of spiritual growth.* Without the help of particular practices it is difficult to become more aware of, and responsive to, God's activity in our lives. Most of us could use guidance on ways of prayer that attune us to God's presence. We may need suggestions for spiritual reading, tips on keeping a journal, or reminders about the nature of authentic humility in self-examination. Perhaps we need someone who has practiced fasting to help us stay on track with our efforts. A spiritual companion can suggest various practices to us as they seem appropriate and help us to discern when or whether to change them. A guide can also help keep us accountable for the disciplines we commit ourselves to.

5. *A spiritual guide will love us and pray for us.* This is probably the most important function of a companion in Christian faith. The love of a spiritual director for the one directed is always mediated by the love of Christ. It is agape love. The ongoing expression of that love is faithful prayer, both within and beyond meeting times. If this is in effect, many inadequacies in a guide can be covered by grace. If it is not present, even virtuoso technique can scarcely make up for it!

Why is it harder to face a person to whom you have broken a promise than to face God?
Ben Campbell Johnson

Styles of Spiritual Direction

There are a variety of patterns in spiritual direction, some quite formal and others much less so. When novices went out to the desert to receive initial training in the Christian life from the elders, the relationship to their spiritual father or mother was one of absolute obedience. The spiritual father or mother had an authority second only to scripture. But it was an authority based on the authenticity of the elder's spiritual life, an authority grounded in love, an authority given them by their novices who were free to leave at any time. The elders had the gift of reading the human heart, and could offer unique words of counsel based on their discernment. This form of spiritual direction is a rarity in the modern world.

In Roman Catholic seminaries, students for the priesthood are required to have a spiritual director. Often the entire faculty is required to provide this direction. There is little choice in the matter, as students are assigned to faculty members. It is an institutional expression of spiritual direction that takes little account of personal gifts or desires. It does, however, reflect the understanding that anyone on a seminary faculty will have sufficient experience with spiritual direction to be able to offer it to a student in the formative phase of preparation for the priesthood. This represents a formal arrangement where the lines of authority are very clear.

Protestants are, for the most part, more comfortable in patterns of relationship without authoritarian overtones. It is still common for the guidance relationship to be "one-way," that is, focused on the spiritual growth of the one seeking guidance. Again, there is a voluntary authority given to the guide by the guided. But it is based on qualities observed in the spiritual guide that are respected by the one who wishes to grow in faith. Essentially, this means that the person seeking guidance trusts the director to be attuned to the presence and movement of the Holy Spirit rather than to mere personal wisdom.

Even in this kind of relationship, there is variation of form. For example, two Christians who are essentially peers, and who respect one anothers' ability to attend to God, may choose to enter a mutual relationship of guidance. In one meeting, one acts as the director and the other receives guidance; in their next meeting, they reverse roles. If they meet for a more extended time, they might even exchange roles during the same meeting.[1] This sort of mutuality expresses well a Protestant emphasis on the "priesthood of all believers." But it may not satisfy those who seek someone they perceive to be "more advanced" on the spiritual journey.

Finally, there are very informal patterns of spiritual guidance that are distinctly mutual and nonprofessional. Some prefer to call these "spiritual friendships." Many of us probably have relationships of this sort already, without thinking of them as forms of spiritual guidance. Prayer partners are basically spiritual friends. Often small covenanted groups in a church provide us with spiritual friends. You may simply have a friend you enjoy talking with about spiritual matters, or someone you turn to for comfort and assurance in times of perplexity and doubt.

The paucity of famous Protestant directors I think refers not to the lack of Protestant spiritual depth but to their focus on the priesthood of all believers, involving countless historically anonymous persons in mutual and informal guidance.

Tilden Edwards

While these are natural and wonderful gifts, it is possible to become more intentional about spiritual friendship. You might choose to develop a friendship you already have by deciding to meet regularly for spiritual conversation and prayer. You might recognize that you have a friend or acquaintance you would like to propose this idea to. It is basically a commitment to travel together on the Christian path of life.

Getting Started with Spiritual Direction

If you think you would benefit from a spiritual companion, the first step is to clarify in your own mind why you want such a relationship. What do you hope to gain from this process? I remember my first experience with spiritual direction in seminary. I had heard about the practice from Roman Catholic friends, and since I was interested in the spiritual life, I thought it was something I should try. The Cenacle sister I met with was a compassionate and experienced director, but I had no clear ideas about what I wanted from direction. Since I had not identified any spiritual issues that might have moved me to seek guidance—only curiosity—I experienced little benefit from our meetings and quit after only three or four sessions. I was not ready for spiritual direction until two years later.

Once you are clear about your reasons for wanting a spiritual mentor, ask yourself what kind of person you would be most comfortable working with. Does it matter to you whether your guide is a man or woman? Are you looking for someone older than yourself? Is it important to you that the person be from your own faith tradition or denomination? How far would you be willing to travel to meet with this person? Most important, what personal qualities are you looking for?

The following personal qualities have become my central criteria for people from whom I seek spiritual guidance. I commend them as general guidelines:

Take five minutes to think through the qualities and characteristics of a person you would seek out as a spiritual guide. List them below.

1. *Look for Christians with a certain maturity of faith.* I want a spiritual mentor to have a wide-ranging experience of life and faith; to be practiced in a life of prayer; to be familiar with the scriptures and some of the spiritual classics; to be knowledgeable about the ways of the human heart; and to have an eye for discerning the "footprints of God."

2. *Look for people who know they are not perfect.* I look for someone who knows human suffering and frailty from personal experience; who is honest about her or his limitations and not afraid to be vulnerable. Humility and compassion for the weaknesses of others are important marks in her or his life. I want a guide whose faith is strong through flexibility rather than rigidity, whose wisdom is practical and salted with humor.

3. *Seek out people who are patient and attentive listeners.* I need a guide who is not easily shocked, who can hear all kinds of feelings, and acknowledge the human reality of all kinds of behaviors without condemnation. I want a guide who can listen to God as well as to me, who is attuned to the promptings of the Spirit when we meet.

4. *Look for people who invite trust.* I want someone who will hold confidences so I can speak freely. I also need to trust my spiritual companion to speak honestly to me about my condition when I am avoiding something I need to face.

5. *Look for mentors who place their trust in the grace of God.* God is the true director of every spiritual encounter. I am not looking for professional competence or confidence in one's own ability apart from the work of the Spirit. I seek someone who is willing to stand before God with me as a forgiven sinner. I want this person's love and prayer for me to be rooted in Christ.

Once you have clarity about the kind of person you are seeking as a spiritual companion, the place to begin is with prayer. Ask God to show you the right person for you to work with. Even if you already have someone in mind, pray for clarity and confirmation. If you have no idea who might be a spiritual guide for you, ask God to reveal or bring someone to you as you are inwardly ready. The Spirit may bring a name, image, or clue into your consciousness in prayer. The Spirit may also act through the suggestion of another person of faith. Seek out recommendations from those you trust.

Start thinking about the people you know. Is there anyone with whom you are already acquainted and to whom you are attracted? If so, bring him or her before God in prayer with complete openness and expectancy. Pay attention to the sense you have of this person in prayer, and to the feelings that surface. If you feel uncomfortable or awkward about asking someone in your cir-

The greatest spiritual guides have been men and women of prayer and quiet, people possessed by an inner stillness of soul, people who are able to guide others because of their own closeness to God.

Kenneth Leech

The great Director of Souls is the Holy Spirit.

Dom Columba Marmion

cle of personal acquaintances to take on this role in your life, attend to the reason. Maybe the person is too close to be objective with you. Perhaps you value your relationship as it is. Maybe it is a professional relationship that would make intimate disclosures uncomfortable or inappropriate. Perhaps the person is too busy, or lives too far away.

When you bring a request of this sort before God, be prepared for the unexpected. You may be led to someone you don't know, or to someone quite unlike yourself. You may well be led to one who does not see him- or herself as a spiritual guide at all. If your initial query is met with resistance because a person feels unprepared for the task, do not lose heart. People who have genuine spiritual gifts are usually humble, ordinary folk who are deeply conscious of their own spiritual struggles and failures. They may be shocked that anyone would consider asking them to act as a spiritual mentor. Yet that sense of inadequacy may be one of the authentic marks of a spiritual guide. You can always ask the person to consider your request in prayer and to be open to the possibility that God is calling you together by the Spirit.

My first spiritual director didn't know he was a spiritual director. He had never so much as heard the term spiritual director, *and neither had I. But our mutual ignorance of terminology did not prevent the work.*
Eugene H. Peterson

It is important that you yourself have a sense of "rightness" about asking a particular person for spiritual guidance. When you receive a willing response, arrange for an initial meeting to explore the possibilities. Talk about your desire for companionship and direction on your faith journey. Indicate why you are seeking guidance at this time. Tell the person that you feel called to explore guidance with him or her in particular. Discuss your hopes and expectations for a spiritual direction relationship. If the person agrees to work with you, set a limited number of meetings (perhaps over a three-month period) in which to establish and test your relationship. This is a time to get more fully acquainted, and to pray for signs of confirmation that God is calling you together in this work before further commitment.

Meeting with a Spiritual Director

When you meet for your first session of spiritual direction, several matters must be decided. What type of relationship do you want? What will be the frequency and length of your meetings? How will you structure each meeting? What kind of evaluation process will you build into your relationship?

The first thing you must do is clarify your mutual hopes and expectations. What does each of you want to receive or offer in this relationship? What does each of you see as the object or goal of your time together? What style of spiritual direction will this be? Is it to be clearly focused on helping *you* relate more fully and freely to God, or is to be a more mutual friendship?

Next, agree on an overall meeting rhythm and time frame. Will you meet every two weeks? Once a month? Take your schedules into consideration, especially if either of you travels frequently. Spiritual direction will bear little fruit if it is not a serious commitment. It will need to take priority over other things at times. Once you have decided on frequency, ask how much time you will give to each meeting. If you meet every week or two, forty-five minutes to an hour may be sufficient. If you meet once a month, an hour to an hour and a half may seem a minimum. I know spiritual companions who live far apart and meet only a few times a year. They spend several days together when they meet, and keep in touch with regular letters and phone calls.

Another practical decision is how to use the meeting time itself. Be clear about your intentions, so as not to waste time that could be focused on your purpose for meeting. You might decide, for example, to give five minutes to small talk (weather, traffic, minor news) as a transition from the immediate experiences of the day into spiritual guidance. It is helpful to begin spiritual direction with several minutes of silence. This allows you both to "center down," clear the surface chatter of the mind, and become aware of divine presence. The silence can be broken by a simple prayer, offered by one or both of you in turn. As the one seeking guidance, you would then begin to share experiences, reflections, and questions with your companion. Your guide in turn would respond with questions, insights, stories, suggestions, or shared experiences. The session might be closed with prayer again. If you offer the opening prayer, you might want your guide to conclude with prayer, or vice versa. In more mutual situations, you might prefer to share both prayer times.

Finally, decide how many times to meet before evaluating your relationship. I recommend committing to at least six meetings for a fair test of how well you work together. The final session will be an opportunity to look frankly at how you experience your relationship, and whether it fits your goals and expectations. If it does, you may choose to renew your commitment for another period of time. If not, you can choose whether to clarify your expectations and restructure your time together or to end the relationship. It should be understood from the outset that either person can terminate the covenant if it is not working well or seems unhealthy in any respect.

Any of these initial decisions about the structure and format of your meeting may change over time as the relationship develops. You may need to explore various options before you discover what works best for the two of you. Some people need more flexible and creative patterns in spiritual guidance than others.

Over the past two years, I have met with a woman spiritual friend one day a month at a convent in the mountains. At first we devised a structured schedule in which each of us had equal time to raise our own issues and have the other listen and respond. But sticking to this time line became strained. As we came to know one another more deeply and to trust the movement of the Spirit between us, we began to give each other whatever time seemed needful. On some days now, only one of us will act as guide to the other. Over time, we try to balance our respective roles as spiritual mentors to each other. This flexibility has evolved gradually and naturally. The one arena we always share in a completely mutual manner is our prayer time, which flows spontaneously back and forth between us until it comes of its own accord to silence. This is the most mutual spiritual companionship I have ever known.

What Do You Talk about in Spiritual Direction?

Many of us have never known a relationship in which we felt comfortable talking about God. Perhaps we grew up in a family where faith was as private as sex, an internal matter one never put public words to. Perhaps religion was a sore topic for our parents, or no topic at all because it was considered fantasy. Maybe we grew up in a church that rigidly forced certain doctrines upon us, and we never felt free to ask our real questions for fear of being ridiculed, harangued, or rejected. Perhaps God simply seemed so awesome that we had trouble saying anything particular about the mystery.

A spiritual companion is someone with whom we can find the freedom and trust to begin exploring who God is in our lives.

What do I actually believe about God? Who is God for me? How does God seem to work in my life? How does God relate to my family, my work, my life in the world? How can I be more aware of God's presence and activity in my daily life? How am I called to respond? These are some of the questions and issues you can expect to explore in a spiritual guidance relationship.

Sometimes we have clear ideas about God and how God acts in our lives. Maybe a transition or impending crisis motivates us to seek spiritual direction. In cases like these, we are likely to talk more about events and relationships, and how God is or is not felt to be present in them. Spiritual guidance is not the same as psychological counseling. Psychological therapies tend to focus on self-image, relationships, or work issues in a problem-solving way. Most do so without reference to God, and that is sometimes the case even in pastoral counseling! Spiritual direction always keeps God in the picture. Your relationship with God is really the heart of spiritual guidance, whatever else you may be dealing with in life.

The primary *relationship in spiritual friendship is between God and the friend, not between the friends themselves.*

Tilden Edwards

Here is a sample dialogue of the kind of conversation that might occur when Pat starts coming to Eleanor for spiritual guidance:

PAT: I feel like I don't know how to pray anymore. I used to pray a lot, and it was very easy. You know, it just came naturally. But for some reason I'm having trouble now. . . . It bothers me. I want to feel close to God.

ELEANOR: Tell me more about your prayer when it came naturally.

PAT: Well, I just talked to God about anything that was on my mind. I talked things out with him as if he were in the room with me, like any other person. That made it easy.

ELEANOR: (*nodding*) So God seemed to be like any other person. Has that changed in some way?

PAT: I think maybe . . . I'm not sure. Sometimes I get really confused about how to think about God. Last month our preacher was saying that the ancient Jews wouldn't even name God because he was beyond all our thoughts or concepts or images. And then I started thinking about that catechism I learned in Junior High School: "God is a Spirit, infinite, eternal, unchanging . . . " I'm beginning to think that I've had a really childish picture of God all these years . . . like some wise old half-ghost who could float through solid objects. I bet this sounds really dumb!

ELEANOR: It doesn't sound dumb. It sounds as if your image of God is changing.

PAT: I guess it is. But I'm not sure I want it to change! Thinking of God as a person made it easy to pray. Now God feels some-how more . . . removed from my life. A God that's like some disembodied spirit just seems so distant. I don't know how to pray to this kind of God.

ELEANOR: What happens when you try?

PAT: Well, I just have this feeling of trying to get my thoughts way out there somewhere, wherever God is . . . and then I think, well, God knows everything already, so why should I be praying anyway?

ELEANOR: What do you associate with the word "spirit"?

PAT: (*long pause*) I guess it makes me think of something insub-stantial, gauzy, not quite real. . . . Oh! . . . Maybe that's it. I feel like God isn't real anymore!

You can see that by attentive listening and a few probing questions, Eleanor has enabled Pat to come to a moment of self-discovery in her prayer life. Pat had not realized that her image of "spirit" translated into "unreality" in her mind. This is the immediate source of difficulty in her prayer life. Eleanor might point Pat toward some other ways of understanding "spirit," perhaps by reflecting on pertinent scripture passages. They can also explore how Pat experienced the reality of God in her life before her image started changing, and where the reality of God is revealing itself to her even now, through the change.

Problems and Potentials in Spiritual Companionship

If you are new to spiritual direction, expect to encounter some of the ups and downs of any close relationship. Remember that in and through this companion, you are dealing with the most intimate and mysterious of all relationships—the one you have with God. There may be relational bumps connected to God or your director, or both!

Sometimes you will feel dissatisfied or irritated with your spiritual mentor. Perhaps you will feel your mentor is not giving you sufficient direction or is being too directive. If you feel this way, you should discuss it openly. There may be good reasons for the approach that bothers you. Your guide may want you to discover something on your own rather than pointing it out to you, or your guide may sense that you need firm directives to counteract certain personal traits that prevent you from responding freely to God. Or, maybe your mentor needs clarification from you on an approach that would be more helpful. If you talk it through, your distress can be part of your learning process.

Sometimes negative feelings toward a spiritual director are really displaced feelings of fear, anxiety, or anger toward God. A sensitive guide can help us see when this is the case. Growing in relationship with God is not easy. We have many defenses against the changes God invites into our lives. Writer Flannery O'Connor warns, "All human nature vigorously resists grace, because grace changes us and change is painful."[2]

Sometimes personality conflicts emerge in spiritual guidance. If these are recognized and dealt with constructively, they can be part of the spiritual growth God brings out of such relationships. A person with a different personality can give us perspectives we would never see on our own. People with opposite characteristics often complement each other wonderfully, each stretching the other to new points of view.

However, it may be that your director really doesn't understand your spiritual journey sufficiently to be of help to you. If you feel that a guide is imposing a personal path that doesn't fit you, and discussion of the matter is no help, then the relationship is not right for you.

There are seasons in all relationships. Some will be short, intense but fruitful. Others will be long-term commitments that evolve slowly and change shape as they grow. There may come a time in the best of spiritual companionships when the guide has offered all she or he can. Then it is time for this particular relationship to end, even though you may continue your friendship by other means.

Finally, it is important to speak of the sexual dimension of spiritual guidance. Especially in male-female relationships, there is always the possibility of sexual attraction turning into sexual

Beginners need counsel to help them ascertain what benefits them most. To this end a director is very necessary, but only a director of experience will avoid making many mistakes and leading souls along without understanding them or without allowing them to learn to understand themselves.

Teresa of Avila (paraphrased)

attachment. If you sense that this movement is taking place, it needs to be brought into the open and talked through. If the dynamic cannot be changed by frank discussion, terminate the relationship. There are absolutely no circumstances in which it is appropriate for sexual behavior to take place within spiritual direction. The boundaries appropriate to your purpose need to be respected.

Testing a Spiritual Companionship

The first several months of a new relationship are the best time to test it. You need to be sure that you are comfortable with your mentor; otherwise you will not feel free to share the deeper issues and concerns of your life in God. Pay attention to your level of trust. Does it deepen quickly over your first several meetings, or is something holding you back? Nagging concerns in the back of your mind are important indicators. Resist the temptation to dismiss them, and examine each one in the light of reason. Is there something that bothers you about this person? Pay attention to your intuitions. "Gut-level" feelings can often alert us to problem areas long before they come to our conscious attention.

I felt a large roominess in his company—a spiritual roominess, room to move around, room to be free. He didn't hem me in with questions; he didn't suffocate me with "concern."

Eugene H. Peterson

The following questions may help you evaluate your relationship with a spiritual director:

Is this relationship helping me to grow in my way of understanding and relating to God? Is it helping me to connect my life and my faith?

When I am with my guide, am I thinking mostly about my life in relation to God, and the spiritual dimension of my other relationships? (If you are thinking mostly about your guide, something is wrong.)

Am I quite comfortable with my guide? Do I expect to be able to open up more and more freely, or is there something disturbing me?

Use common sense when you are testing out a person's ethical sensibilities. It helps if the spiritual guide you are considering or evaluating comes with unreserved recommendations from people you know and trust.

The Value of Spiritual Guidance

There may be times in your life when a spiritual guide is invaluable to you, and times when you do not need such a relationship. Sometimes the general teaching and preaching of the church is sufficient to our need. Sometimes we find the direction we are seeking from books. Teresa of Avila acknowledged centuries ago that when we cannot find a living Christian to guide us, we can rely on good spiritual books. The authors of spiritual classics, whether ancient or modern, are often excellent guides.

Small groups in the church—Bible study groups, experiential learning classes, or covenant groups—serve to direct and support us in our spiritual journeys. Para-church groups such as Twelve-Step programs, Marriage Encounter, and Cursillo (Protestant adaptations include Walk to Emmaus and Tres Dias) have been life-changing for many thousands. Small groups are more accessible to many people than individual spiritual guidance and should be openly explored. They can be fine sources of guidance.

Still, as the voices that opened this chapter remind us, there are times when what we really yearn for is one other person who can give us concentrated time and attention. We may need someone with more experience, or simply someone with an outsider's objective perspective on the spiritual concerns we struggle with. The fruits of such a companionship in faith can be tremendous. We can come to name God's grace in our lives and to understand our own experiences of faith. New ways of praying and offering our lives in service to God can be explored. We can find ourselves personally affirmed and loved even when we confess our deepest needs and vulnerabilities. We are supported in our practice of spiritual disciplines and held accountable to a flesh-and-blood human being. This is how one man described the benefits of his spiritual mentoring:

> I have discovered personal support for my journey. Not only have I been accepted, affirmed, appreciated, and given words of assurance about God's work in my life, but I have known the incalculable support of prayer from a man who knows me and who cares about God's work in my life. I no longer feel alone in my struggle.[3]

Spiritual companionship in the Christian life is a precious grace. Our journeys are not meant to be utterly solitary. Trying to be faithful to God can be a lonely and trying path. We need each other. We grow best in community. Saint John of the Cross put this truth into an eloquently simple statement four centuries ago: "God has so ordained things that we grow in faith only through the frail instrumentality of one another."[4] May we find joy in being such instruments for one another!

Notes

1. For a personal illustration of this kind of mutual guidance relationship, see Ben Campbell Johnson's fine little book, *To Pray God's Will: Continuing the Journey* (Philadelphia: Westminster Press, 1987), chap. 5.
2. Sally Fitzgerald, ed., *The Letters of Flannery O'Connor—The Habit of Being* (New York: Vintage Books, 1980), 308.
3. Johnson, *To Pray God's Will*, 90.
4. Cited without reference in editor's introduction, *Weavings* 2, no. 4 (July–August 1987): 3.

8 Entertaining Angels Unawares
The Spirit of Hospitality

Come, you that are blessed by my Father, inherit the
kingdom prepared for you . . . ; for I was hungry
and you gave me food, I was thirsty and you gave me
something to drink, I was a stranger and you
welcomed me.

Matthew 25:34–35

I had just graduated from college three months before. My
mother had earned a precious sabbatical, and we were taking the
trip of a lifetime, starting in Scotland. On this particular day, we
had left Edinburgh to venture into the Scottish countryside. The
legendary Highlands were carpeted in heather and chill mist. By
the time our bus arrived in the isolated town where we would
spend the night, darkness had fallen and it was pouring rain. The
bed-and-breakfast we had arranged to stay in was already full.
With no access to a telephone, we were simply given the name
of another house to try. A cab dropped us in front of a home with
no lights on. It was late and cold. Our legs and suitcases were drip-
ping by the time we reached the door.

A pleasant but surprised couple answered our knock. When
we asked for accommodations, they explained apologetically
that they already had a boarder for the night. Our faces must have
fallen as low as our spirits. Where would we go at this hour in
such a downpour, in a tiny hamlet that seemed to have folded up
for the night? They told us to wait inside the door. We heard muf-
fled voices consulting. A few moments later, we were being
ushered with quiet smiles into a cozy and pleasant room. Grateful
and relieved beyond telling, we didn't ask questions. We sank,
exhausted, into deep sleep in a comfortable double bed.

Next morning, the woman prepared a sumptuous Scottish breakfast for us: fruit juice, eggs, kippers, toast, butter, jam, and tea. It was not until we were packed and ready to leave that we discovered the extent of our hosts' generosity. With guest quarters already occupied, this couple had given us their own bedroom. They had slept in the living room.

The experience is etched in my memory. This couple cheerfully sacrificed their comfort to meet our need. Not a hint of sullenness or resignation shadowed the act. It was a simple, straightforward expression of hospitality—the first of many such experiences on that trip. When I came down with a fever in Italy, the woman whose pension we stayed in brought my mother a large bowl of expensive fruits to help me regain my health. It was a gift from the heart. On more than one occasion we received extraordinary generosity from total strangers.

It has been my experience that those of modest means are often the most willing to share what they have. A friend recently told of a trip to Mexico during which her group attended a village church for worship. Afterward, they were besieged with invitations to village homes for the Sunday meal. My friend knew that several families had pooled their meager resources to put on a feast. They cooked the one chicken they had and insisted that their guests take the best portions. My friend felt a mixture of wonder, gratitude, guilt, and humility. Her hosts offered what they had with joy and festivity. She received the meal as an act of pure generosity and fellowship.

What are your most vivid memories of receiving hospitality? of offering it?

Hospitality in Jewish and Christian Tradition

It is hard for us to comprehend, but hospitality in the ancient Near East was originally offered to complete strangers. People who appeared from the unknown might bear gifts or might be enemies. Because travel was a dangerous venture, codes of hospitality were strict. If a sworn enemy showed up at your doorstep asking for food and shelter, you were bound to supply his request, along with protection and safe passage as long as he was on your land. All sorts of people had to travel at times through "enemy territory," which meant that hospitality to strangers was a matter of mutual survival. It was a kind of social covenant, an implied commitment to transcend human differences in order to meet common human needs.

It is not surprising, then, that hospitality was a hallmark of virtue for ancient Jews and Christians. But in scripture, hospitality reflects a larger reality than human survival codes. It mysteriously links us to God as well as to one another. Abraham and Sarah's hospitality to the three angels at Mamre unseals God's promise of a son in their old age (Gen. 18:1–10). The angels are representatives of God's own presence. In a phrase echoing their story, the author of Hebrews urges, "Do not neglect to show hospitality to strangers, for thereby some have entertained angels unawares" (13:2, RSV). Hospitality in biblical times was understood to be a way of meeting and receiving holy presence. Although providing hospitality was risky, it was a risk taken in faith. After all, the stranger just might be an angel—a messenger of God!

For Christians, the risk was seen as an opportunity to meet a singular stranger, the Risen Christ. Jesus made it clear that whatever kindness or neglect we show to "one of the least" of his brothers or sisters, we do to him. "Oft, oft, oft goes the Christ in the stranger's guise," says an old Celtic rune. Christian hospitality finds classic expression in the Rule of Saint Benedict: "All guests to the monastery should be welcomed as Christ, because He will say, 'I was a stranger, and you took me in.' "[1]

Can you name an incident in your life where you felt you met Christ in the guise of a stranger?

Professor of mission and evangelism Mortimer Arias tells us that the remarkable explosion of Christianity in the first century was due not only to proclamation of the gospel, but to the extraordinary quality of Christian hospitality. It evidently so impressed one Roman emperor that he commanded his provincial governors to begin practicing hospitality like that of the Christians, if they wanted their empire to grow and remain civil. There must have been a quality of mutual respect and love in those early Christian communities that created hospitable space for very different kinds of people to enter and find a spiritual home. Arias calls that attractive character of early Christianity "centripetal mission" or "evangelization by hospitality."[2] There was, for many, something irresistibly enticing about a community that *saw Christ* "in friend and stranger." Those outside the circle were drawn in like leaf tendrils to light.

Christ in quiet, Christ in danger, Christ in mouth of friend and stranger.

Saint Patrick's breastplate

The Essence of Hospitality

> Hospitality means receiving the other, from the heart, into my own dwelling place. It entails providing for the need, comfort, and delight of the other with all the openness, respect, freedom, tenderness, and joy that love itself embodies.

What is the essence of hospitality for you? Write down your own definition.

That is how I like to describe the nature of hospitality. The *other* can be literally anyone apart from ourselves. Ancient practices of hospitality had particular application to strangers and enemies. This is a challenging notion for us today, but one that deserves our attention. Who are the "strangers" and "enemies" in our midst: immigrants? people with AIDS or TB? people who differ from us in ethnic origin, religious conviction, or political affiliation? Do adolescents in general, or our own teenagers in particular, feel at times like complete strangers to us?

Our "dwelling place" may be physical—a room, apartment, or house. It may also be a metaphor for mental and emotional "space." We can invite others into our inner world of thoughts and feelings, sharing gifts of heart and mind. Gracious inner space gives others room to play, question, and converse; room to be heard and understood; room to reveal themselves as they choose.

Hospitality is essentially an expression of love. It is a movement to include the guest in the very best of what we ourselves have received and can therefore offer. It is the act of sharing *who we are* as well as *what we have*. Thus, hospitality of heart lies beneath every hospitable act. The classic elements of hospitality offered to guests are food and drink, shelter and rest, protection and care, enjoyment and peace. These paired categories cover a basic range of physical, emotional, and spiritual needs. They reveal that hospitality is concerned with the total well-being of the guest.

What do you think the most important ingredients of hospitality are? Take a few minutes to write your response.

In offering shelter, nourishment, rest, and enjoyment to our guests, we often discover that they gift us with their presence. The relationship of host and guest is a mutual one; "the very root of the word 'hospitality' . . . *hospes* means both host and guest."[3] The uncanny sense of receiving more than we give applies to many situations. I once telephoned an acquaintance who was dying from cancer, wanting to offer what solace I could. The conversation completely reversed my expectations of who was ministering to whom. I received a powerful witness to Resurrection faith from a man who was full of joy and amply prepared to face his Maker.

122

God's Hospitality to Us:
Gift and Grace

Hospitality begins with God. Because we have a supremely hospitable God, in whose image and likeness we are made, we are capable of reflecting hospitality back to God, to others, to the earth, and even to ourselves. Hospitality to strangers does not come easily to us. Until we are deeply rooted in knowledge of God's grace, we have neither the living example nor the strength of commitment to live hospitably in a hostile world. Whatever form our hospitality may take, it is already a response to God.

God's first great act of hospitality to us is Creation itself. "In the beginning" God made a home, a dwelling place for creatures of the Divine Hand. And what a home it is! In the language of Genesis, it is a garden of delight, filled with every conceivable provision: food, shelter, beauty, and peace. All is gift—given to us for nourishment and joy, and given into our care to tend.

The most basic image of God's hospitality in creation is food. It is no accident that sharing food is the primary expression of hospitality in human culture. Theologian Alexander Schmemann notes that "centuries of secularism have failed to transform eating into something strictly utilitarian. Food is still treated with reverence. A meal is still a rite—the last 'natural sacrament' of family and friendship."[4]

In Orthodox theology, the physical matter of creation was, for human beings, a means of spiritual grace and communion with God. We were to respond in gratitude and blessing. Yet, on the heels of Creation came the Fall. The intended communion between God and human beings through creation was lost. What went wrong?

One could say that we chose to receive gifts of hospitality without thanking or even acknowledging the Host. We tried to provide for ourselves rather than to receive provision from God. We even made every effort to become Host of the universe in God's place! It was a tragic breach of relationship—an undisguised denial and rejection of divine love.

But God's love did not leave us in our self-invited exile. For Christians, the second great act of divine hospitality is the Incarnation: "The Word became flesh and dwelt among us." It is a rather inconceivable thing that God should come among us *in person* to forgive, reconcile, and restore human creatures to the communion God intends. In fact, the apprehension of God-in-

> *The Creator God has spread out for our delight a banquet that was twenty billion years in the making. A banquet of rivers and lakes, of rain and sunshine, of rich earth and of amazing flowers, of handsome trees and of dancing fishes, of contemplative animals and of whistling winds, of dry and wet seasons, of cold and hot climates . . . and so are we, blessings ourselves, invited to the banquet.*
>
> *Matthew Fox*

> *If the divine power of heaven had preserved its dignity by not coming into contact with diseased humanity on earth, then our sickness would not have received its cure and we would not have been healed. But God assumed human life from birth unto death . . . healing "all that lies between."*
>
> *Todd H. Speidell*

123

Christ was so momentous to the early Christians that Paul could only describe the mystery as *New Creation*. The *first* Creation and the *new* Creation provide us with a framework for comprehending the immensity of divine hospitality to us.

God-in-Christ enters "enemy territory," a society of people so immersed in rebellion and delusion that they no longer recognize or acknowledge him. Into such an estranged world, the Holy One can only come as stranger—one unrecognized, unsought, and unloved by most of those to whom he came.

How do I experience God as a "stranger" in my life? in the life of my culture?

Why would God—the Holy, Righteous, and Pure—choose to enter the messy circumstances of our perverse and distorted humanity? Evidently the divine eye sees through a different lens than we expect. It is not that God doesn't perceive with crystal clarity the terrible travesty of our sin. But God seems to see even the greatest evils of which we are capable as mortal wounds. God sees the ugliness of our sin with the eyes of the Great Physician who yearns to heal. God feels the tragic consequences of our alienation with the heart of the Good Shepherd who suffers compassion.

God-in-Christ . . . opens the closed door of righteousness from within. . . . He brings the unrighteous in instead of talking to them through the closed door. . . . He thus spends his life . . . and finally pours out his very blood for the hardened, the dejected and the hostile.

Karl Barth

If we can discern motives for God becoming human, they are to be likened to the monastic practice in the Middle Ages of hospitality to travelers and wayfarers that developed into caring for the sick. Modern hospitals and hospices embody the legacy of these earlier Christian ministries. Like the merciful Samaritan of Jesus' parable, God steps into our situation and stoops to tend the deadly wound of our sin. "Those who are well have no need of a physician, but those who are sick," says Jesus to the Pharisees. "For I have come to call not the righteous but sinners" (Matt. 9:12, 13).

The lengths to which God will go to heal us are fully revealed on the cross. A costly divine forgiveness lies at the heart of New Creation hospitality. Jesus' arms stretched on the beam—extended to release our sin, to receive all in love, to invite us to new life—are the very image of God's unaccountably gracious hospitality to us. On the cross, Jesus lives out his own parable of the father whose open arms gladly receive back a wayward child. Recall how the father in that story throws a lavish feast to celebrate his son's restoration to the family! Such a heart represents the essence of divine hospitality. In Baptism God opens the door to the family house and says, "Welcome home, my child!"

How do I experience the hospitality of God? of Christ? of the Spirit?

In the Eucharist, God brings us to the dinner table and cries, "Eat! Eat! I made it especially for you!"

God-in-Christ has received us into his own dwelling place, where we find in plenty all we have need of: forgiveness, healing, reconciliation, comfort, peace, joy, communion—abundant life for body and soul. Could there be any hospitality to match that of the Host of Heaven?

Our Hospitality to God: Receptivity and Response

To speak of our hospitality to such a God is humbling, for no response seems adequate. It is not in our power to make "adequate" responses. God asks only that we offer whatever love and gratitude we have in us. In the upside-down order of grace, the more we empty out our love to God the more we are filled with it.

Our first act of hospitality to God is to *receive* what God gives. How distressing for God to offer grace so freely, only to have us refuse or ignore it! We have devised many excuses for closing the door on divine love. We allow ourselves to become distracted and preoccupied so we are not even aware of the value of God's gifts. We decide that we are unworthy to receive anything from God, so refuse the gift. We convince ourselves that we must first prove worthy of receiving something, so spend our days trying to *earn* what can only be *received*. It takes genuine humility to receive God's gifts. This simple truth is illustrated in the following story from the desert wisdom tradition:

Can you identify some ways in which you "close the door" on God's gifts to you? Do you find it hard to receive gifts from others? Hard to give gifts? Why?

> Once some of the elders came to Scete, and Abba John the Dwarf was with them. And when they were dining, one of the priests, a very great old man, got up to give each one a little cup of water to drink, and no one would take it from him except John the Dwarf. The others were surprised, and afterwards they asked him: How is it that you, the least of all, have presumed to accept the services of this great old man? He replied: Well, when I get up to give people a drink of water, I am happy if they all take it; and for that reason on this occasion I took the drink, that he might be rewarded, and not feel sad because nobody accepted the cup from him. And at this all admired his discretion.[5]

I often cry out that we are worthy of compassion for being content with so little. God has infinite treasures to give us. . . . God's grace is like a torrent. When it is stopped from taking its ordinary course, it looks for another outlet. . . . Let us . . . make way for grace.

Brother Lawrence

When we become willing to receive from God, we will naturally express the hospitality of gratitude. Adoration, thanks, and blessing are the most fitting way to receive the Holy One hospitably into our inner "dwelling place." Every expression of trust, praise, and joy delights our God. Gratitude expands our hearts, creating space for God and others.

What is the place of gratitude in your own spiritual journey right now?

We offer hospitality to God when we make ourselves consciously present to the Divine Presence and listen for what the Spirit is communicating. The story of Jesus with Martha and Mary (Luke 10:38–42) offers a striking illustration. We usually think of Martha as the one who offers hospitality to Jesus and his disciples. Does she not invite them into her home and busy herself with much serving? We tend to assume that Mary "does nothing but sit" and listen passively to a charismatic Jesus. We have imagined that the story pits service against prayer, action against contemplation.

But Mary *chooses* to sit and listen to Jesus. In doing so, she lays aside the traditional role her culture and sister expected of her. Is her choice not also an act of service to Jesus? He came to preach a message, to proclaim God's kingdom, to invite conversion of life. Jesus yearned for people who would hear his words. Mary chooses to receive the gift of Jesus' presence with her own presence, to receive his message with her hearing. Is it possible that Jesus experienced Mary's listening as a deeper act of hospitality than the provision of food and drink?

Listening attentively to the great Other is a service of hospitality. God has a deep and passionate desire for us to listen to the divine word. This word is our life-source, our means of communion with One whose love we are destined to share. God wants fellowship with us! Every means by which we allow ourselves to be present, to listen, and to be encountered by the Holy One is a form of hospitality.

What kinds of hospitality do you offer directly to God? What would you like to be able to offer?

Finally, however, listening implies obedience. The hospitality of attentiveness remains stillborn unless joined by the hospitality of acting in accord with what is heard. To *do* the will of God is the ultimate expression of receiving the holy Other into the inner sanctuary of our hearts and the larger temple of our lives. Hospitality to God is finally expressed in our intentions and actions toward every creature God loves. We are not permitted to separate our love for God from our love for others.

Our Hospitality to One Another: Compassion and Community

Our love for one another is a direct expression of our love for God: "those who do not love a brother or sister whom they have seen, cannot love God whom they have not seen." (1 John 4:20) One of our more persistent problems is that we do not *see* each other as sisters or brothers, much less love each other as such.

> An ancient Rabbi once asked his pupils how they could tell when the night had ended and the day was on its way back. "Could it be," asked one student, "when you can see an animal in the distance and tell whether it is a sheep or a dog?" "No," answered the Rabbi. "Could it be," asked another, "when you look at a tree in the distance and tell whether it is a fig tree or a peach tree?" "No," said the Rabbi. "Well, then what is it?" his pupils demanded. "It is when you look on the face of any [person] and can see . . . your brother [or sister]. Because if you cannot do this, then no matter what time it is, it is still night."[6]

What does it take to see in *every* other person a sister or brother? If we cannot truly accept our weaknesses as well as our gifts, we will be unable to love others in their brokenness and giftedness.

We are speaking once again of humility. A humble heart is hospitable. It accepts people as they are—a mix of familiar and unfamiliar, good and bad. Acceptance leaves others free to be themselves in our dwelling place. It does not require them to be like us. Our guest may be friend or total stranger, mentally impaired or emotionally estranged, different in race, faith, social circumstance, or political perspective. Hospitality means giving all guests the freedom to reveal themselves as they choose. A guest should not need to fear personal attack, rejection, or conversion efforts on the part of the host. *Freedom* is the medium of human exchange in true hospitality.

I recall an occasion when my family, en route to Florida for vacation, was invited to stay overnight with acquaintances. It was at the height of the Vietnam war, a war my college-age brothers were strongly opposed to. During the course of dinner conversation with our host family, the subject of the war arose. When my brothers rather naively voiced their sentiments, the table fellowship immediately palled. Clearly our hosts disapproved of my brothers' views. Their capacity to make us feel welcome

The love of neighbor . . . means . . . meeting "our neighbors truly and honestly only as lost ourselves, i.e., exactly as we are, and not in the role of saviors. . . . " God shows us our neighbors as brothers and sisters.
Todd H. Speidell

as guests was affected by this difference. The gracious home with all its amenities was no longer hospitable space.

The practice of hospitality cannot depend on shared views or values. When we impose or imply such conditions, we are offering entertainment rather than Christian hospitality. We must learn to value the strangeness of the stranger, as community-building consultant Parker Palmer points out:

> Hospitality means letting the stranger remain a stranger while offering hospitality nonetheless. It means honoring the fact that strangers already have a relationship—rooted in our common humanity—without having to build one on intimate interpersonal knowledge, without having to become friends.[7]

This perspective goes against the grain of American culture. We sometimes seem determined to produce friends with friendliness. Perhaps the idea of the stranger is so threatening that we can scarcely conceive of any value in strangeness. Yet the very unfamiliarity of the stranger is a means through which we gain new perspective on our too-familiar lives. One who is different can shake us loose from stereotypes and false convictions. We need to preserve room for the stranger in our hospitality.

Sometimes we experience the shock of encountering a hidden side in someone we have known for years. Changes in attitude and behavior can make strangers out of spouses or close friends. It is most disorienting to find someone with whom we live or work becoming a personal enemy. Practicing hospitality with our nearest and dearest can be as challenging as with complete strangers!

I have spoken of the risk involved in offering hospitality to strangers. There is also risk in refusing hospitality. We may miss God's gift. Had they not invited the stranger to enter their lodging and sup with them, Cleopas and his friend (Luke 24) would have missed recognizing their traveling companion as the risen Christ!

Practicing hospitality of heart has implications for every common dimension of our lives. It affects our homes, workplaces, neighborhoods, schools, churches, and ways of being public citizens. A few possibilities are sketched below; I encourage you to add your own creative reflections.

. . . people do not enter our lives to be coerced or manipulated, but to enrich us by their differences, and to be graciously received in the name of Christ.

Elizabeth Canham

Benedict says, "Be here; find Christ in the restless teenager, demanding parent, insensitive employer, dull preacher, lukewarm congregation." . . . create a hospitable space for whoever and whatever God sends into [your] lives now.

Elizabeth Canham

Hospitality at Home

There is a very real sense in which hospitality "begins at home." Family relationships are the first place to put the art of Christian hospitality into practice. Children are not personal possessions, but sojourners in our homes. They belong to God, who entrusts them to our care through their growing years. Providing safety and love are essential to the internal hospitality of family life. Yet security is balanced by allowing increased freedom over time, appropriate to each child's capacity and level of development.

Parents provide a hospitable home by being genuinely present to their children—available to listen, affirm, guide, and correct. Taking time to listen and talk to one another is one of the most important expressions of hospitality in home life, especially in an age when time is at a premium. It requires self-sacrifice on the part of adults to make this a priority.

Are children free to learn from their mistakes in your home? Parents can be clear that certain behaviors are not acceptable (physical aggression, lying, stealing, cheating), while making it equally clear that each child is loved and accepted as a person. Making distinctions between the person who chooses and the behavior chosen is important. When our children make poor choices, we can let them know that we trust them to be capable of better ones. Hospitality leaves room for change and growth.

How do you respond when your childrens' aptitudes and values differ from yours? You love classical music and your teenager lives for hard rock; you're an outdoor enthusiast and your child prefers the company of books. Parents who affirm each child's unique personality and gifts offer hospitable space to little ones who seem at times like strangers in our homes. Since children in the same family can be vastly different from one another, parental affirmation of diversity also helps children accept the differences between themselves.

Family life involves the daily interactions of people with different desires and agendas living in common space. Conflicts inevitably occur. Learning to forgive the daily scrapes and bruises that result from bumping up against one anothers' interests is a central expression of hospitality. Forgiveness is a direct sharing of

God's hospitality to us. It frees us from the bondage of resentment and desire for retribution. It frees us from anxiety and constraint. Forgiveness opens the door to renewed care and concern for each other, clearing a path for healed and healthy relationships.[8]

Playing with children is an expression of hospitality, for it offers the gift of delight and joy. From making up stories to camping ventures, play is important to the child in all of us. We need times of sheer fun and silliness, times for a little "divine madness" to liven us with levity. Laughter and play enlarge the soul.

When adult relationships in a home embody presence, acceptance, affirmation, forgiveness, and playfulness, there is plenty of room for children, friends, and strangers to enter comfortably into family life. By contrast, when these adult relationships are marked by self-interest, controlling behavior, unresolved conflict, and anxiety, very little hospitality can be offered to anyone—inside or outside the family.

The quality of hospitality *within* family relationships profoundly impacts the hospitality offered to those outside. My husband and I have sometimes visited friends who seem to enjoy triggering each other's sensitivities in our presence. Each tries to gain our sympathy against the spouse. As friends and guests, it is a most uncomfortable position to be placed in. There is no room for us to be ourselves nor, in truth, to be with them. There is only room to take sides in a chronic power struggle.

Author Wendy Wright suggests that families can express the original vision of hospitality to strangers in a variety of ways. One way is through adoption, especially of hard-to-place children who have siblings, disabilities, or mixed racial background. Another might be sheltering a homeless couple, a pregnant teen, or a young person estranged from his or her family. It can be an act of hospitality to take in a foreign student or a foster child for a period of time.[9] Each family needs to decide, under the leading of the Spirit, what forms of hospitality are appropriate to its circumstances.

Hospitality in the Workplace

A central expression of hospitality at work is listening openly to others' ideas, concerns, and critiques. Hospitality means being receptive to good ideas, whether they come from a mail clerk or a senior vice president.

If you have an office door, leave it open at regular intervals. Indicate your willingness to welcome others into your work space. It signals that you value the thoughts and questions of your co-workers. You will doubtless need time for work when you are not available to others as well. Keep a balance.

Is the physical ambiance of your workplace inviting or sterile? Consider what you might do to make it more welcoming. Good lighting and functional equipment are important. Is your furniture comfortable and invitingly arranged? Small touches like plants and pictures add pleasure for the eye and heart.

Honoring appropriate boundaries in common work areas is an act of hospitality. Do not enter another person's work space too often or without good reason. In work areas without separate rooms, avoid loud or prolonged conversation. Be courteous in your language; even humor can be used to mock or exclude certain people.

In meetings, actively encourage (but do not force) the participation of those who are more reticent. If you tend to talk willingly or you hold a position of authority, deliberately withhold your speech in order to leave room for others to speak.

If you are a supervisor or manager, you have more power to make the workplace hospitable. Aim to create an organization that allows employees to grow both personally and professionally. Be sure people have access to the information they need to do their jobs. Build an environment of trust and credibility, rather than fear and suspicion. Keep in touch with your employees, offering encouragement, appropriate praise, and constructive suggestions. Be careful not to overload your employees with meetings and committees; give them sufficient time to do their work.

Hospitality in the Neighborhood

In typical neighborhoods today, residents know only their immediate neighbors; the rest are virtual strangers. Work patterns, frequent moves, and individualism all contribute to our increasing isolation from one another. How can we help make our neighborhoods welcoming places?

Make the effort to become acquainted with your neighbors. Neighbors who trust each other can offer many small courtesies that make residential areas safer and more hospitable. You need not be close friends to watch one another's homes or feed pets when a neighbor is away from home.

Take time to listen to a lonely neighbor. Many older people live alone, or with a spouse who needs sustained care. To be able to unburden anxiety or relieve boredom through conversation is a real help. There are a few "stay-at-home moms" in my neighborhood who crave adult company while caring for small children. When I am especially busy, it is a real discipline for me simply to offer the hospitality of ten minutes of attentive listening.

Single parents feel the burden of working and raising children alone. You might offer to watch the kids for an evening, freeing your single neighbor to do necessary errands or enjoy a movie without having to pay a sitter.

If you like to organize, throw a block party to help people on your street get acquainted. Invite everyone to cook up their favorite dish to share, or set up grills in a central yard for a big cookout. Plan games for the kids and get parents involved in supervising them.

Parker Palmer suggests canvassing the neighborhood for an "inventory of talents." Are there people on your street with special skills or hobbies they would be willing to share with neighbors, either freely or in exchange for a different talent? Someone might want to share carpentry skills with a person who could take care of their mending pile. Others would be happy to change the oil in your car for the love of being a "grease monkey." When people are willing to share their talents and services with neighbors for the sheer joy of it, hospitality has taken root in the neighborhood!

When a street is cordoned off, refreshments provided, music and games offered by the neighbors to each other, and people are given an excuse to mingle for a few hours on a summer evening, then the street takes on new and more hospitable meaning. Do it often enough and that street becomes a place where people pass each other with warm memories and hopeful expectations rather than unawareness and suspicion.

Parker J. Palmer

Hospitality in our Churches

Of all places, Christian churches ought to be supremely hospitable. As the Body of Christ, the church is called to reflect the hospitality God has shown us in Jesus. Is your church a hospitable community? Here are some questions to help you evaluate.

How does your church welcome visitors and newcomers? Does your church convey the spirit of an open, receptive community or a closed social clique?

How does your church make its own members welcome? Are every person's gifts honored in the community? How are weaker members of the "family" supported and encouraged? How does the community respond to those who depart in some way from social expectations, and who therefore struggle to find a community of love and acceptance: people with physical handicaps or learning disabilities, people who suffer from mental or emotional illness, divorced people, gay and lesbian people?

How constructively does your church deal with conflict? Like families, every church has its share of discord. Because we differ from one another in temperament, personality, upbringing, and conviction, we will come to loggerheads over certain decisions. How much room is there for theological disagreement in your church? Do people feel free to express their deepest convictions without fear of being personally attacked or rejected? Hospitality does not require us to agree with one another; it requires that we offer free space for speaking and listening.

Is your listening to one another encompassed by a deeper listening to God? In the church, our trusting invitation to receive the clarity of the Spirit should be the container for our hospitality to other peoples' beliefs and interpretations.

Does your church practice the "passing of the peace"? If so, is it understood as an occasion to share the peace of Christ that enables us to transcend differences and be reconciled to one another in love?

Does your church see intercessory prayer as a form of hospitality to others? When we intercede for others in prayer, we welcome them into our inmost sanctuary of compassion. We participate in the spacious hospitality of God's grace for each person. Since hospitality has a special place for the stranger, praying for our enemies (inside or outside the church) is a most fitting expression of the heart's hospitality.

How does your faith community receive its pastors? Your pastoral leaders need your love, encouragement, and prayer as much as you need theirs. Many priests and ministers feel isolated, embattled, overwhelmed, and inadequate. They never feel they have enough time to meet all the demands of church life, let alone respond adequately to family or personal needs. Guilt over lack of a personal prayer life is common.

Here are a few simple acts of hospitality you could offer to the leaders we invest with great expectations and responsibilities. Listen to your pastors. Find out what a typical work week is like. Ask if they take a regular day off. Do they have sufficient time for personal spiritual nurture to sustain the service of their ministry? Ask what kind of support you can offer that would enable them to continue a growing and vital spiritual life. Then give them the support they need. Pray for your church leaders, during worship and through the week. Invite your pastor (and family) to your home occasionally for enjoyment and fellowship.

Finally, how does your church offer hospitality to those who never enter its sanctuary? Do you provide overnight facilities to the homeless? meals for the hungry? prison visitation, or support for the families of prisoners? a home for new refugees? What we do for the least, we do for our Lord.

Civic Hospitality

Hospitality in our larger social communities finds expression in the structures of human society and governance. Are the basic resources of our common life—homes, schools, medical care, and recreation—widely available? Perhaps we need to work for zoning regulations in our neighborhood that ensure housing options for people of various income levels. We can work for clean, safe parks that are located within walking distance of various neighborhoods. Community programs in sports, recreation, and arts that encourage healthy child and family activity are an important form of civic hospitality.

How hospitable are our schools? Do we need to work for alternative ways of funding schools to ensure more equitable distribution of educational resources? How hospitable is our educational process? Highly competitive classrooms create a hostile and intimidating learning environment for most students. "Knowledge" is an external commodity to be digested like lunch, and "learning" in such settings is often little more than conforming to a teacher's expectations. Hospitable education allows students to discover and express the understandings they already have. It encourages learners to connect their life experience with larger questions, issues, and perspectives. Teachers can welcome students into classrooms where they are given freedom to explore and express their growing understandings in safety and peace.[10]

Many Americans, especially those who are recent immigrants or who are poor and undereducated, are not registered to vote. Can we ensure that all who are eligible to vote are registered and have the basic information to make informed choices? Are voting sites accessible to the whole community?

Does your town have a "welcome wagon"? These organizations are effective in orienting newcomers to the resources and

When pastor André Trocmé was once asked why he inspired an entire French village to risk giving shelter to Jews during World War II, he replied simply, "I could not bear to be separated from Jesus."

When we look at teaching in terms of hospitality, we can say that the teacher is called upon to create for . . . students a free and fearless space where mental and emotional development can take place.
Henri J. M. Nouwen

services of the community. They also encourage new residents to become active in areas of public concern that interest them.

Our discussion of hospitality would not be complete without including the natural world. Many other creatures, upon whom we depend more than we know, inhabit this planet with us. The results of our exploitation of nature have never been so grievously apparent. If hospitality means receiving the *other* into our own dwelling place with freedom, respect, and joy—if it means welcoming strangers in our midst and providing for their need, comfort, and delight—then what does it mean with respect to God's other creatures? How can we be hospitable to the inhabitants of the earth whose dwelling places we are rapidly crowding out and despoiling? We must give serious attention to this question if we wish to be hospitable to God, who created all living things and a world sufficient in provision for every kind.

Rooted and Grounded in Love

Do some aspects of civic hospitality sound more like "social justice" than "hospitality"? Hospitality to the stranger is, in truth, a way of "doing justice." The biblical meaning of justice is simply "right relationships" with one another. Showing kindness to the wayfarer, supporting the widow and orphan, taking in the homeless poor, and offering hospitality to strangers—these were expressions of just relations with the neighbor in scripture. They remain so today, even in a more complex society.

We are no doubt afraid of some forms of hospitality. They seem naive and unrealistic in a society that has become violent and dangerous. Certain expressions of hospitality are more risky than others. We need to make choices based on what we believe God is calling us to do for the sake of Christ.

Our hospitality is rooted and grounded in God's hospitality to us in Christ. Until we know this love deep in the core of our hearts, we will have neither courage nor trust to share hospitality with others in more than superficial ways. Christian hospitality is a risk taken in faith. It is an act of sacrificial joy offered in the full light of the risen Christ, a light that transforms our perspective on everything.

As we learn to receive God's hospitality to us, we will become more hospitable to God, to each other, and to our fellow creatures. This will make us a different kind of community. Others will see something enticing in us. Perhaps they will even say "See how they love one another!"

Notes

1. *The Rule of St. Benedict*, trans. Anthony C. Meisel and M. L. Mastro (Garden City, N.Y.: Image Books, 1975), 89. See chapter 53 in *The Rule* for Benedict's vision of receiving Christ in the guest.

2. Mortimer Arias, "Centripetal Mission or Evangelization by Hospitality," *Missiology: An International Review* 10, no. 1 (1982): 69–81.

3. Parker J. Palmer, *The Company of Strangers: Christians and the Renewal of America's Public Life* (New York: Crossroad, 1986), 69.

4. Alexander Schmemann, *For the Life of the World: Sacraments and Orthodoxy* (Crestwood, N.Y.: St. Vladimir's Seminary Press, 1973), 16.

5. Thomas Merton, *The Wisdom of the Desert* (New York: New Directions, 1960), 70.

6. Printed in "Social Concerns Newsletter from the Passionists," Union City, N.J.

7. Palmer, *Company of Strangers*, 68.

8. Forgiveness is a thorny topic in family life, and more complex than a single paragraph can describe. For example, where there is no recognition of fault and no serious repentance, forgiveness on the part of the offended party is not likely to open the relationship for healing. For more on this important subject, see *Weavings* 7, no. 2 (March–April 1992), which is devoted to the theme of forgiveness.

9. See Wendy M. Wright, *Sacred Dwelling: A Spirituality of Family Life* (New York: Crossroad, 1989), 60. Motives become important here. Some people have taken in foreign students for the summer in order to exploit their labor, and some parents take in foster children in order to receive state funding.

10. Clearly, this refers to the ambiance of learning created by the teacher's own attitudes and manner. If the external reality of a school is dominated by violence and security issues, the possibility of real education is the first casualty. For an excellent discussion of hospitable teaching, see Parker J. Palmer, *To Know as We Are Known* (San Francisco: Harper & Row, 1983). See also Henri J. M. Nouwen, *Reaching Out* (New York: Doubleday & Co., 1975), 58–63.

9 Putting It All Together
Developing a Rule of Life

As our lives and faith progress, the heart expands and
with the sweetness of love we move down the paths
of God's commandments. Never departing from His
guidance . . . we patiently share in Christ's passion, so
we may eventually enter into the Kingdom of God.
The Rule of Saint Benedict

Certain kinds of plants need support in order to grow properly.
Tomatoes need stakes, and beans must attach themselves to sus-
pended strings. Creeping vines like clematis and wisteria will grow
on any structure they can find. Rambling roses take kindly to garden walls, archways, and trellises. Without support, these plants
would collapse in a heap on the ground. Their blossoms would
not have the space and sun they need to flourish, and their
fruits would rot in contact with the soil. We would be unable to
enjoy their beauty and sustenance.

When it comes to spiritual growth, human beings are much
like these plants. We need structure and support. Otherwise our
spirituality grows only in a confused and disorderly way. The fruit
of the Spirit in us gets tangled and is susceptible to corruption,
and the beauty of our lives is diminished. We need structure in
order to have enough space, air, and light to flourish. Structure
gives us the freedom to grow as we are meant to.

There is a name in Christian tradition for the kind of structure that supports our spiritual growth. It is called a *rule of life*.
Without a rule of life, very little of what you have been reading
and exploring in this book will prove to be of lasting value to you.
This final chapter is an opportunity for you to begin putting
together what you have learned. It is time to make some choices
concerning the spiritual practices you feel called to engage in.

*It is unlikely that we will deepen our
relationship with God in a casual or
haphazard manner. There will be a
need for some intentional commitment
and some reorganization in our own
lives. But there is nothing that will
enrich our lives more than a deeper
and clearer perception of God's
presence in the routine of daily living.*
William O. Paulsell

What Is a Rule of Life?

A rule of life is a pattern of spiritual disciplines that provides structure and direction for growth in holiness. When we speak of *patterns* in our life, we mean attitudes, behaviors, or elements that are routine, repeated, regular. Indeed, the Latin term for "rule" is *regula*, from which our words *regular* and *regulate* derive. A rule of life is not meant to be restrictive, although it certainly asks for genuine commitment. It is meant to help us establish a rhythm of daily living, a basic order within which new freedoms can grow. A rule of life, like a trellis, curbs our tendency to wander and supports our frail efforts to grow spiritually.

Throughout Christian history, those who have been serious about maturing in the spiritual life have embraced discipline. Remember that discipline means training and practice. Author William Paulsell notes that while we tend to resist the whole idea of discipline, we have to admit that it allows us to make the most of our God-given gifts:

> Athletes, musicians, writers, scientists, and others progress in their fields because they are well-disciplined people. Unfortunately, there is a tendency to think that in matters of faith we should pray, meditate, and engage in other spiritual disciplines only when we feel like it.[1]

Finally, the purpose of a rule is to help us grow into holiness. God calls us to be holy as God is holy, to grow into greater intimacy with the One we are created to resemble: "Beloved, we are God's children now; what we will be has not yet been revealed. What we do know is this: when he is revealed, we will be like him, for we will see him as he is" (1 John 3:2). A rule of life allows us to cultivate and deepen this growing likeness. It fosters gifts of the Spirit in personal life and human community, helping to form us into the persons God intends us to be.

Yet this gradual transformation into the full image and likeness of God does not happen automatically. It is not a process of natural growth, like that of a sapling into a fully mature tree. It is a process that requires the death of much that seems natural to us, in order to allow a deeper mystery of our life in God to rise up. Maturation in faith is like the metamorphosis of a caterpillar into a moth. The caterpillar must yield up the life it knows and submit to the mystery of interior transformation. It emerges from this process transfigured, with wings that give it freedom to fly. It is naturally attracted to light, although still vulnerable to ruin if deceived by artificial light. A rule of life gives us a way to enter the lifelong process of personal transformation. Its disciplines help us to shed the familiar but constricting "old self" and allow our "new self" in Christ to be formed—the true self that is naturally attracted to the light of God.

There are both corporate and personal rules of life in Christian tradition. Perhaps the best known of all corporate rules is that of Saint Benedict, attractive and practical because of its moderate tone and commonsense wisdom. The Rule of Saint Benedict describes both attitudes and specific practices to guide monks in their common life. Personal rules are formulated by individuals to help them receive and express more fully the gifts of the Spirit. They are very diverse, reflecting the needs and spiritual aspirations of those who devise them. Some focus more on developing inner attitudes, values, and habits such as humility, charity, faith, and gentleness. Others emphasize specific practices such as prayer, fasting, and self-examination. These, of course, are meant to lead us toward the inner attitudes mentioned, as well as to their outward expression in human community.

We are about to open a school for God's service, in which we hope nothing harsh or oppressive will be directed. For preserving charity or correcting faults, it may be necessary at times, by reason of justice, to be slightly more severe. Do not fear this and retreat, for the path to salvation is long and the entrance is narrow.
The Rule of St. Benedict

Examples of Personal Rules

When Pope John XXIII was a seminary student, he included the following elements in his rule:

Fifteen minutes of silent prayer upon rising in the morning

Fifteen minutes of spiritual reading

Before bed, a general examination of conscience followed by confession; then identifying issues for the next morning's prayer

Arranging the hours of the day to make this rule possible; setting aside specific time for prayer, study, recreation, and sleep

Making a habit of turning the mind to God in prayer

A very different style of rule was developed by Catherine de Hueck Doherty, the Russian baroness who founded Madonna

House in Ontario, Canada. Drawing on the Russian hermit tradition, she recommends a monthly retreat into silence and solitude for a twenty-four-hour period. A hermitage (*poustinia* in Russian) is a simple cottage isolated from human traffic that allows for fasting, prayer, and immersion in scripture.

Dorothy Day, who began a ministry called "houses of hospitality" for the poor in New York, had another kind of personal rule. She received the Eucharist daily, read the Bible daily, and kept a journal that was, for her, a form of prayer. She saw Christ in the faces of the poor.

Martin Luther King Jr. developed a rule to guide the nonviolent protests of the civil rights movement. His rule emphasized the spiritual principles and inner attitudes undergirding one's actions, although it also included specific practices like meditation, prayer, and service. Every demonstrator had to agree to this rule:

Meditate daily on the teachings and life of Jesus.

Remember always that the nonviolent movement in Birmingham seeks justice and reconciliation, not victory.

Walk and talk in the manner of love, for God is love.

Pray daily to be used by God in order that all might be free.

Sacrifice personal wishes in order that all might be free.

Observe with both friend and foe the ordinary rules of courtesy.

Seek to perform regular service for others and the world.

Refrain from violence of fist, tongue, or heart.

Strive to be in good spiritual and bodily health.

Follow the directions of the movement and the captains of a demonstration.[2]

It should be clear from these few examples that there can be great latitude in a personal rule of life. Your rule will be unique to your personality, circumstances, and needs, yet in harmony with the basic historic practices of Christian life and faith through the centuries. Developing a personal rule is a matter of discernment.

Making Choices

If you are like me, you will by this time either be very excited by all these possibilities for spiritual growth or you will feel over-whelmed. I am typically tempted to think that I must do every-thing, all at once! But this is humanly impossible, unless you are a monk or solitary who has intentionally devoted your entire life to the practice of spiritual disciplines. As people who live in a world of families and work commitments, we must choose what seems most central and what is genuinely feasible for us. How do we go about making such choices, especially if they all seem good?

The first thing to do is pay close attention to what you feel most attracted to. Go back over the chapter headings in this book. Look at the "Invitations to Explore" sections in chapters 2, 3, 5, and 6 and the practical suggestions in each chapter. Are there cer-tain suggestions you feel especially drawn to? Is there anything that seems to "have your name on it"? Write down what comes to mind.

Next, ask yourself why you are attracted to a given discipline. Does it seem suited to your personality? Does it represent an area of growth you feel in need of at this point in your life? Does it promise a measure of balance in your life you do not currently enjoy? Are you simply attracted inwardly for reasons that are not apparent at the moment?

We are often attracted to spiritual practices that seem natural to our personality. For example, a more introverted person might be drawn to the more inward disciplines of contemplative prayer and self-examination. An extrovert might be attracted to com-munal expressions of worship and hospitality that suit a more interactive nature. There is nothing wrong with choosing spir-itual practices because they feel congruent with who you are. They are likely to be the disciplines you engage in with the great-est consistency and satisfaction. They may not, however, be the practices that will stretch you toward the greatest growth or the ones you most need. Still, they are probably a good place to get started, especially if you have little spiritual discipline in your life at the moment.

Perhaps you are drawn to a practice because it promises to bring greater balance to your life. You need to be whole to be healthy. The Christian spiritual life expresses our entire being, for the Spirit is concerned with every dimension of human life, individually and in community. Perhaps precisely because you are an introvert, God is calling you to open yourself to a community spiritual practice. You need to develop the relational side of your spirituality because it is too easy for you to sink comfortably into inward and private reflection. Or precisely because you are an extrovert, God is inviting you to look inward, and you should pay attention to the motives and needs behind your desire to constantly interact with others.

Look closely at the practices described in this book that do *not* appeal to you, or may even repulse you. Bring the matter into your prayer. Why do you feel such resistance to this particular discipline? Does God have anything to say to you about it? A strong negative reaction to a practice such as fasting or self-examination may reveal that you are resisting paying attention to a part of your life in need of healing. Ask God to show you what spiritual disciplines you need in your life right now. You may be surprised by the response!

The Rule of Saint Benedict views balance in human life very seriously. Times of common and private prayer are balanced. The daily rhythm of monastic life provides a balance of exercise for spirit, mind, and body: prayer, study, and manual labor. We need to consider such balance as we choose disciplines to structure into our daily lives. Each of us needs a balance between personal and corporate disciplines; each of us need practices that help us look to our own hearts, and practices that help us forget ourselves in meeting the needs of others. When the Spirit is freed to do its work, these disciplines work together in a mutually sustaining way.

To summarize, there are three basic questions to reflect on in choosing disciplines for your rule of life:

What am I deeply attracted to, and why?

Where do I feel God is calling me to stretch and grow?

What kind of balance do I need in my life?

When, after thinking about these questions, you are clear about your priorities, you need to ask what is realistic for you to commit to. This is a matter of honoring personal limitations. Far better to commit to a single practice and stick with it than to take on five and quit altogether because you cannot keep up. The spiritual life is not a heroic achievement. It is a matter of gradual growth in faithfulness. Realistic commitment is an expression of humility.

Take account of your personal character. Some of us respond well to clear structure, while others of us flourish best with more flexibility. Some of us wake up filled with energy at five in the morning; some of us are wide-eyed and alert at midnight; some of us find our peak energies somewhere in the middle of the day. God deserves our best energy, not the dregs. Choose times for spiritual reading and prayer with this in mind.

Take account of your personal circumstances at this point in your life. If you are a parent staying at home with preschool children or an adult child now tending aging parents, an hour of concentrated spiritual practice daily is probably unrealistic. You may want to try short periods of reflection on a scripture verse throughout the day, or a breath prayer carried into your routines. You might find it helpful to practice a simple self-examination before bedtime, observing where you have felt God's presence in your family life and how you have responded to this grace.

If you have a demanding job with long hours of work, it may make sense to consider what forms of hospitality you can offer to God and to others in that setting. Prayers of the heart are a good way to remember the divine presence through your day. You may need to schedule a personal retreat several times a year for more in-depth opportunities in prayer and meditation.

If you are retired, perhaps you have more freedom to choose how much time you devote to spiritual practices. Thirty to sixty minutes of spiritual reading and prayer might be quite feasible. If your health is good, you could practice a weekly fast. Opportunities to offer hospitality may abound.

A chronic illness or disability can be either an opportunity or an impediment to prayer, depending on its nature and degree. If you are very sick, your capacity for concentration will be diminished. It is best to stick with short, simple phrases of prayer, and perhaps invite others to read short portions of scripture to you. If you are not too sick, your limited mobility gives you a real opportunity to spend time in spiritual reading, prayer, and self-examination. You can exercise a genuine ministry of intercession, and offer hospitality of heart in many ways, including writing letters to those who would appreciate a word of encouragement or friendship.

Whatever your circumstances, it is always possible to include some form of spiritual discipline in your daily priorities. If you want to become and remain physically healthy, you eat sensibly and exercise regularly. If you want to become spiritually healthy and remain replenished, you practice spiritual disciplines regularly. It is that simple.

Keeping Ourselves Accountable

Once you have decided on a rule of life you can realistically give yourself to, write it down. Commit yourself in print. Remember, this is not a once-for-all-time decision, but a rule of life that is practical for this time in your life. Put a copy of your rule in a place where you can review it frequently, perhaps near your place of prayer.

Choose one person you love and trust to share your rule with. Ask that person to pray for you, and to help hold you accountable to faithfulness in your practice. If you have a spiritual friend, or decide that you will seek a spiritual director, this is the natural person to share your rule with. But a prayer partner or other friend in faith could also serve in this role. A small group seeking spiritual growth together can be an excellent help in this regard. Spouses and other family members should know enough of your rule to be able to encourage, or at least not interfere needlessly with, your practice. The better part of wisdom suggests that you *not* expect your spouse to be the primary person holding you accountable in your spiritual life.

It is very important to seek support from your faith community when you decide to become serious about developing your spirituality. The Christian life is dangerous terrain to travel alone. We get easily discouraged when our disciplines become boring or difficult. We become distraught when they do not produce the results we expected. We are subject to confusion in our practices in part because we are just learning them, and in part because of our own distorted perceptions and personal limitations. Any spiritual discipline can be manipulated for our own ends rather than offered as a means of God's transforming grace in us.

We need the wider community of faith to help us stay on track. That community comes to us through corporate worship, study, and service, and through the grace of individuals whose experience and wisdom can guide our own. We will find only loneliness and illusion if we insist on forging the path alone. The Body of Christ is given to us for mutual encouragement, support, clarity, guidance, and love. To receive that gift in all humility is an experience of grace.

I hope it is very clear by now that the spiritual life in Christian practice is a joint intention. It joins the personal and the corporate: our individual disciplines need to be practiced in the context of a community of believers if they are to glorify Christ. It joins the inner and the outer: the disciplines that search and speak to our own hearts must be balanced by disciplines that engage us in self-forgetful service to others if they are to bear fruit in God's kingdom.

Finally, the Christian spiritual life joins the divine intent for us with our own intent to love and serve God more completely. Our desire to know the Lover of Souls more intimately is far outweighed by a divine passion to draw us into the eternal, tender embrace of holy love that is our created destiny. Because our God is patient and faithful, we can offer our stumbling, inconsistent efforts at a rule of life and know they will be accepted. As long as our desire is true and we are willing to persist despite many stalls, detours, and breakdowns, God' grace will strengthen us to persevere. The goal is infinitely worth all the effort, confusion, and pain along the path:

> For this slight momentary affliction is preparing us for an eternal weight of glory beyond all measure, because we look not at what can be seen but at what cannot be seen; for what can be seen is temporary, but what cannot be seen is eternal.
>
> 2 Cor. 4:17–18

It is my prayer that you will have found something in these pages to encourage and guide your spiritual quest. The practices described are means of grace, paths to the food and drink we crave in our inmost being. God can use them to nourish us. Together they offer a true soul feast. Since you cannot indulge in a feast all at once, but only in courses and over time, I trust you will choose and savor each food for the unique nourishment and delight it can give. Resist the temptation to be greedy at this table.

O, Begin! Fix some part of every day for private exercises. . . . Whether you like it or no, read and pray daily. It is for your life; there is no other way: else you will be a trifler all your days. . . . Do justice to your own soul; give it time and means to grow. Do not starve yourself any longer.

John Wesley

Its bounty will not be depleted by many hungry seekers. Indeed, the more the children at this table, the greater the abundance of supply. God's economy is not based on scarcity. The richest sources of spiritual nurture are permanently set upon the table of our lives. While it would be folly to ignore or refuse them, there is no need to rush or grab. Take and receive as you have need. Enjoy each to the full.

> Oh, taste and see that the Lord is good!
> Happy are those who take refuge in God! (Ps. 34:8)[3]

Notes

1. William O. Paulsell, "Ways of Prayer: Designing a Personal Rule," *Weavings* 2, no. 5 (November–December 1987): 40.
2. See Paulsell, "Ways of Prayer," 43. In his book *Rules for Prayer* (Mahwah, N.J.: Paulist Press, 1993), Paulsell indicates that these "Ten Commandments" are found in Martin Luther King, Jr.'s book *Why We Can't Wait* (New York: Signet Books, 1964).
3. *Psalms for Praise and Worship: A Complete Liturgical Psalter*, eds. John C. Holbert, S. T. Kimbrough, Jr., and Carlton R. Young (Nashville: Abingdon, 1992), 57.

Appendix A
Group Study Guide

The following questions for reflection and suggested exercises are intended to help small groups or classes work through the material in each chapter. The book can be used for a ten-session study in one of several ways: (1) Begin your study with a gathering for personal acquaintance and group sharing; then work through each of the nine chapters in turn. (2) Begin by working through the chapters, assigning the introduction and first chapter's reading in advance of your first meeting; then add a meeting at the end to evaluate your group process and plan how to follow up on areas of key interest. (3) Work through each chapter in turn, giving two sessions to chapter 3, one on prayer as communication and one on prayer as communion. By combining these suggestions you can use the book over twelve meetings.

There are probably more questions and exercises listed under each chapter than can be adequately explored in any given group or class session. You will need to select the suggestions that seem most appropriate or interesting to your group. The chapter on worship has more reflection questions than any other. Numbers six through nine are really more detailed explorations of number five. Any one of these questions could form the basis for an entire class or small group session. You might decide, for example, that you would like to follow this study with another that would focus on hymns, songs, and spirituals, or a study devoted entirely to the sacraments and how they are interpreted and practiced in various Christian traditions. Pay attention to what parts of your discussion are most animated and the kind of sharing that elicits the most intense interest. These may suggest what your group would like to follow up with further study or experiential activity.

Chapter 1: Hunger and Thirst for the Spirit

1. What indications of spiritual hunger and thirst do you perceive in our time? What do you see as the reasons for this hunger? Take time to share, as you choose, your own stories of spiritual yearning.

2. Discuss the terms piety, devotion, and spirituality. How do you respond to each of these words? What associations, positive or negative, do they hold? Look together at the following definintions of spirituality from contemporary writers:

   Spirituality is our self-transcendent capacity as human beings to recognize and to participate in God's creative and redemptive activity in all creation. [Suzanne Johnson, *Christian Spiritual Formation in Church and Classroom*, p. 22]

   A spirituality is a walking in freedom according to the Spirit of love and life. This walking has its point of departure in an encounter with the Lord. [Gustavo Gutierrez, *We Drink from Our Own Wells*, p. 35]

   Spirituality is the pattern by which we shape our lives in response to our experience of God as a very real presence in and around us. . . . To be spiritual is to take seriously our consciousness of God's presence and to live in such a way that the presence of God is central in all that we do. [Howard L. Rice, *Reformed Spirituality*, pp. 45–46]

   How do you respond to these definitions? How would each of you define spirituality for yourself? What makes a spirituality Christian?

3. Talk about "discipline" and your personal associations with this term. Why is discipline important? What are its limits? How do you respond to the idea of spiritual disciplines?

4. Look together at the margin exercises under "Tradition" on page 13. What does the word *tradition* evoke? Do you think there is a difference between tradition and convention? If so, how would you characterize the difference?

5. Take time to identify and reflect on the reservations or anxieties you may feel about exploring the spiritual life more deeply. All feelings, both of attraction and resistance, are important to acknowledge. They do not need to be resolved, only noted and appreciated.

Chapter 2: Chewing the Bread of the Word

1. What is your typical way of reading? What kind of reading do you approach in an "informational mode," and what kind in a "formational mode"?
2. Discuss your understanding of the nature of scripture. In what sense is it God's Word? How do you respond to the metaphor of the lake on page 19? Does the reverse perspective of iconography make sense to you as a description of the way God's Word works on us? Try out the exercise on page 20 together.
3. Talk about *Lectio Divina* and its phases. Do some stages seem more familiar or comfortable than others? Which parts do you think you might need encouragement and support for? Did any of you try out the process after reading this chapter? What did you discover?
4. Are there other kinds of written materials that you naturally read and respond to in a way similar to *Lectio Divina*? What types of spiritual reading beyond scripture are you attracted to (devotional reading, fiction, poetry)? Share with one another the books or sources that have been especially helpful in deepening your own spiritual life.

Chapter 3: Communication and Communion with God

1. Begin by sharing with the group each person's perceptions of what prayer is. For instance, how would you define it? What is most central about your own understanding and practice of prayer?
2. Discuss communication in prayer. Share with one another how you try to listen to God, and how you sometimes "hear" God. Are there certain avenues through which you seem more receptive to God's communication?
3. Talk about honesty in prayer. Did you grow up with certain assumptions or unspoken rules about what was "allowable" to say to God? How do you respond to the Psalms as a vehicle of prayer?
4. Share your beliefs and uncertainties concerning intercessory prayer. What experiences with petition and intercession have led you to pray as you do now? Take a look together at

the various ways of describing what happens when we pray (see "Views of Intercessory Prayer," page 38). Which best express your understanding, and why?

5. Did anyone explore a new way of engaging in communicative prayer (imaging intercession, writing or paraphrasing a psalm, journaling a conversation from scripture; see pages 41–44)? If so, share your experience to whatever extent you are comfortable in doing so.

6. Had you ever considered prayer as a form of communion? Can you trust that God enjoys your company? Do you find yourself attracted or resistant to contemplative prayer?

7. Discuss impediments to your prayer. What distracts you outwardly and inwardly? How do you cope with these blocks and interruptions?

8. The relationship of prayer is essentially one of transformation. How do you feel about the possibility of being changed by God in the relationship of prayer? What do you want changed? What do you not want changed?

9. If anyone explored a contemplative prayer path (prayer of presence, prayers of the heart; see pages 46–49), share what you experienced, to whatever extent you are comfortable. Arrange to have one member of your group lead the rest in a prayer of presence (see pages 46–47) as a closing exercise. Whoever reads should be sure to give plenty of pause and space for people to enter into the experience.

Chapter 4: Gathered in the Spirit

1. Does Kierkegaard's "theater of worship" shift your notion of what worship is? Do you think it is important for people of faith to gather for worship? Why or why not?

2. How many of you feel guilty when you take time out to relax? Do you give yourself permission to keep Sabbath? Take five minutes to list the commitments and activities in your life at this time. Divide them into three categories by asking, What is necessary? What is desirable? What is neither? For each commitment, ask yourself whose expectations you are trying to meet (yours, others', God's). Make a choice to let go of something. Ask someone else in the group to support your choice with prayer.

3. Share with one another your overall experience of corporate worship. In what ways does it feed you? What do you yearn for that you do not experience?

4. Did you try the self-examination suggested in the margin on page 61, or any other ideas for enlivening worship from this chapter? What effect, if any, did it have on your experience of public worship?

5. It is often a mystery what moves us at any given time. Are there aspects of worship that frequently move you to a sense of divine presence? Does the Word more often come alive for you through music, prayer, preaching, silence, or sacrament?

6. Music expresses an intuitive, sensory, and affective side of our being. What is the role of sacred music in your own worship experience? What are some of your favorite hymns and songs? What makes them special? Are there songs or hymns you just can't bear? Why?

7. Out of the crucible of African American slavery came the rich tradition of "spirituals" that speak of the unquenchable faith enabling people to not only endure but transcend pain with praise. What are your favorite spirituals? Take a look in the index of several recent hymnals to see what spirituals are included. Are you surprised at how many of our most popular hymns are spirituals? Sing one or two as a group, and talk about what they have come to mean to you.

8. How do you experience the sacraments in worship? What does Holy Communion mean to you? Has its significance changed for you over time? Do you yearn for "something more" in sacramental life? If so, can you name it?

9. "Rituals, like stories, emerge from and speak to our intuitive, emotional consciousness. . . . When worship becomes too intellectual or wordy, it loses its depth and significance" (John Westerhoff, *Bringing Up Children in the Christian Faith*). What do you think about this statement? What role does ritual play in your spiritual life? What about silence?

10. What is your feeling about postures and gestures appropriate to worship? Would you like more freedom of movement in worship, or are you comfortable with things as they are? What would give you the freedom to use different gestures?

11. What kinds of visual or sensory aids do you find conducive to worship (candlelight, symbols, banners, pictures, icons, fragrance, sounds, etc.)? How important is it to you to include the senses in worship? What suggestions are you comfortable with?

Chapter 5: The Practice of Self-Emptying

1. What images are associated with fasting for you? What are your reactions to the idea of fasting as a spiritual discipline? Discuss especially any anxieties or reservations you have.
2. How does your group respond to the notion of Lenten fasting as a spiritual springtime? Do you believe that limits can be life-giving? See how many examples of this principle you can think of in life.
3. Does anyone in your group have experience with regular fasting? Invite people to share whatever experiences they have had, whether for physical, moral, political, or spiritual reasons. Do you think the motive behind a fast affects your experience of it?
4. Discuss the concept of abstinence in relation to our North American consumer culture. Reflect together on the margin quotes by Gerald May and William Ralph Inge on page 76.
5. Look at the alternative forms of "fasting" suggested on pages 76–77. Which of these seems most significant to you? Let your group brainstorm ideas to add to the list. How do you understand the relationship between food fasting and other forms of fasting?
6. Commit to try the exercise described in the lower margin on page 77. Find a prayer partner in your group to encourage and support your practice until your next meeting.
7. What do you think of the connection between fasting and repentance? Do you feel drawn in any way to take up the invitation in this section (page 79)? How would you go about it?

Chapter 6: Of Conscience and Consciousness

1. Talk through your feelings about confession. What histories do you have with this word? How has it been used or misused in your families and churches? Why do you think

that serious and specific confession has fallen into such disuse?

2. Take a look at the two basic truths described under "Points of Departure" (page 84) and the exercise in the margin of page 84. Talk about your responses.

3. Does anyone in your group have experience with regular self-examination? If so, perhaps that person would be willing to share in general terms how the practice is helpful.

4. Did anyone in your group try out the suggested margin exercise on page 90? If so, share reflections on that process. In general, how do you feel about the idea of using the Ten Commandments or the Beatitudes as an aid to self-examination?

5. Have you ever confessed a serious weakness to a trusted friend? How does this idea strike you? Talk about the natural fears and embarrassments that tend to prevent us from taking such a step. Whom do you trust with your sins?

6. Clarify with one another the differences between "examination of conscience" and "examination of consciousness" as you understand them. Do you find one pattern more attractive than the other?

7. Did you try one of the two practices described under "Invitations to Explore" on pages 94–96? If so, share your experience of the process (you need not reveal content unless you choose to).

8. Discuss the section on a true spirit of confession. What keeps self-examination healthy? What distinguishes genuine from false humility?

Chapter 7: Companions on the Journey

1. Have you ever felt, or do you currently feel, a need for companionship on your faith journey? Who has been a companion for you in the past? Is there someone who serves this role now, formally or informally?

2. Do you remember as a child finding the hidden objects in line drawings? Learning to see the hidden grace of God in daily life is something like this game. What kinds of circumstances or people help you to notice the hidden workings of God?

3. As you look through the key elements of spiritual direction on pages 104–105, which ones do you respond to most deeply?
4. Discuss the various styles of spiritual direction. Which do you feel more comfortable with?
5. What criteria would be most important to you in seeking a spiritual guide? What kind of personality, gifts, or traits would you look for? Make a group list.
6. How do you respond to the sample conversation of spiritual guidance on pages 112–113? Can you imagine yourself talking with someone about your prayer life or your images of God in this way?

Chapter 8: Entertaining Angels Unawares

1. Share with others your most vivid experience of receiving hospitality. Then share your most satisfying experience of offering hospitality.
2. What seem to you to be the most essential ingredients of hospitality? What is the difference between hospitality and entertainment?
3. Have you ever felt you met Christ in a complete stranger? Talk about the idea of offering hospitality to strangers. What is attractive and what is frightening about it?
4. Share incidents in your life in which the expected role of host and guest, giver and receiver, were reversed. Were you comfortable with the reversal?
5. Share with one another your experiences of God's hospitality to you.
6. Talk about how you offer hospitality to God. How well are you able to receive, to listen, to respond?
7. Who are the strangers and enemies in our lives today? What would offering them hospitality look like? What would make it possible to do so, in your estimation?
8. Discuss the practical ideas for hospitality at home, church, workplace, and in the civic arena. Which of these seem most important? most practical? What ideas can your group contribute?

Chapter 9: Putting It All Together

1. At this final meeting take time at the beginning to share with the others what has been most significant for you in the course of this study.
2. Discuss the place of structure in our lives. Why do we need it? How much do we need? When does it get in the way, and when does it facilitate the way?
3. Talk about the differences you see between natural growth and spiritual transformation (see pages 138–139). How do you understand the purpose of a rule of life?
4. Look through the "Examples of Personal Rules" section. Which of those described is most attractive to you, and why? How would you want to structure your own rule?
5. The following is a process that will take at least half an hour. Pair up with another person in the group whom you trust and respect. Reflect on any decision making you may have done concerning the practices you need or desire in your life at this time. Share your thinking and discernment with each other. Discuss especially your responses to the three questions on page 142. Talk about how your priorities, personality, and circumstances affect realistic choices. Let your partner reflect affirmation or questions back to you. Reverse roles. Ask each other to pray for continued guidance, discernment, and strength of commitment. Promise support and encouragement to one another in specific ways beyond this meeting time: for example, brief notes, telephone calls, prayer, or periodic meetings.

Appendix B
Sources and Authors
of Marginal Quotations

Chapter 1

Howard L. Rice, chaplain and professor at San Francisco Theological Seminary. *Reformed Spirituality: An Introduction for Believers* (Louisville: Westminster/John Knox Press, 1991), 7.

Augustine, Bishop of Hippo, North Africa, 354–430 A.D. *Confessions*, X, 27. As quoted in *The Lord of the Journey: A Reader in Christian Spirituality*, ed. Roger Pooley and Philip Seddon (London: Collins, 1986), 73.

Chapter 2

Macrina Wiederkehr, author, member of St. Scholastica Benedictine Monastery. *A Tree Full of Angels: Seeing the Holy in the Ordinary* (HarperSanFrancisco, 1991), 53.

John Calvin, French reformer, largely based in Geneva, 1509–1564. *Institutes of the Christian Religion*, ed. John T. McNeill (Philadelphia: Westminster Press, 1960), 1. 6. 3, p. 73.

John Calvin, *Institutes*, 1. 7. 4, p. 79.

Macrina Wiederkehr, *A Tree Full of Angels*, 53.

Macrina Wiederkehr, *A Tree Full of Angels*, 53–54.

Dietrich Bonhoeffer, German Lutheran theologian opposed to Hitler, 1906–1944. *The Way to Freedom*. Letters, Lectures, and Notes 1935–1939. In *Collected Works of Dietrich Bonhoeffer*, vol. 2, ed. Edwin H. Robertson; trans. Edwin H. Robertson and John Bowden (London: Collins, 1966), 58–59.

Chapter 3

Maria Boulding, contemplative nun of Stanbrook Abbey, England. *The Coming of God* (Collegeville, Minnesota: The Liturgical Press, 1986), 7–8.

Flip Wilson, American comedian.

Douglas V. Steere, Quaker author and former emeritus professor of Haverford College. *Dimensions of Prayer* (New York: Women's Division, Board of Global Ministries of the United Methodist Church, 1962), 23.

Søren Kierkegaard, Existentialist Danish religious philosopher, 1813–1855. *Christian Discourses,* trans. Walter Lowie (Oxford: Oxford University Press, 1940), 324.

George MacDonald, Scottish clergyman, novelist, and poet, 1824–1905. *Diary of an Old Soul* (London: George Allen & Unwin Ltd., 1905), 96.

Rubem Alves, Professor of Philosophy, State University of Campinas, São Paolo, Brazil. *I Believe in the Resurrection of the Body* (Minneapolis: Fortress Press, 1986), 19.

James Outram Fraser, missionary to Lisuland, Southwest China, 1886–1938. In Mrs. Howard Taylor, *Behind the Ranges: A Biography of J. O. Fraser of Lisuland* (London: OMF, 1970), 111.

Frances Dominica, Dominican prioress, *Prayer* (Oxford: The Amate Press), 15.

Douglas V. Steere, *Dimensions of Prayer*, 80.

Alfred Lord Tennyson, Poet Laureate of England, 1809–1892. "Idylls of the King: The Passing of Arthur," from *The Norton Anthology of English Literature*, 4th ed., vol. 2 (New York: W. W. Norton & Company, 1979), 1206.

Ann Belford Ulanov, Professor of Psychiatry and Religion at Union Theological Seminary, New York City. *Picturing God* (Boston: Cowley Publications, 1986), 164.

Brother Lawrence of the Resurrection, French Carmelite lay brother, 1611–1691. *The Practice of the Presence of God*, trans. E. M. Blaiklock (London: Hodder & Stoughton, 1981), 45.

Walter de la Mare, French poet, 1873–1956. "The Secret," from *The Complete Poems of Walter de la Mare* (London: Faber & Faber, 1969).

Theophan the Recluse, Russian Bishop and Staretz (elder), 1815–1894. *The Art of Prayer: An Orthodox Anthology*, compiled by Igumen Chariton of Valamo, trans. E. Kadloubovsky and E. M. Palmer (London: Faber & Faber, 1966), 109.

Theophan the Recluse, *The Art of Prayer*, 89.

Henri J. M. Nouwen, Dutch priest, noted author and spiritual leader. *Behold the Beauty of the Lord: Praying with Icons* (Notre Dame: Ave Maria Press, 1987), 13–14.

Thomas Merton, Trappist monk and eminent spiritual writer of twentieth century, 1915–1968. From an address to nuns in

California, quoted in M. Basil Pennington, *Centering Prayer* (Garden City, N.Y.: Doubleday Image Books, 1982), 56–57.

Robert L. Faricy, American Jesuit, professor of Spiritual Theology in Rome. *Praying for Inner Healing* (London: SCM, 1979), 75.

Chapter 4

Augustine of Hippo, *Expositions on the Book of Psalms* (LF VI, 178) on Psalm 138:2.

William Temple, Archbishop of Canterbury, 1881–1944. Quoted in Richard J. Foster, *Celebration of Discipline*, 158, without source.

Jamie Phelps, Professor of Systematic Theology at Catholic Theological Union in Chicago. From "Black Spirituality" in *Spiritual Traditions for the Contemporary Church,* ed. by Robin Maas and Gabriel O'Donnell (Nashville: Abingdon, 1990), 342.

Thomas H. Troeger, Professor of Preaching and Communication at Iliff School of Theology. Verse 2 of "As a Chalice Cast of Gold." From "Borrowed Light" by Thomas H. Troeger; copyright and reproduced by permission of Oxford University Press, Inc.

John S. Mogabgab, editor of *Weavings: A Journal of the Christian Spiritual Life.* From *Weavings,* 4, no. 4 (July–August 1989): 3.

Isaac Pennington, early member and proponent of Society of Friends (Quakers), 1617–1680. Quoted without source in D. Elton Trueblood, *The People Called Quakers* (Richmond, Ind.: Friends United Press, 1966), 91.

Avery Brooke, Episcopal lay teacher and writer. *Plain Prayers in a Complicated World* (Boston: Cowley Publications, 1993), 135.

Paul Waitman Hoon, former Professor of Pastoral Theology at Union Theological Seminary, New York. *The Integrity of Worship* (Nashville: Abingdon, 1971), 329.

Fred Pratt Green, contemporary hymn text writer. Verse 1 of hymn, "When in Our Music." Copyright 1972, Hope Publishing Co., Carol Stream, Ill. Used by permission.

Chapter 5

Dallas Willard, professor at School of Philosophy, University of Southern California. *The Spirit of the Disciplines: Understanding How God Changes Lives* (HarperSanFrancisco, 1988), 167.

Dallas Willard, *The Spirit of the Disciplines,* 169.

Alexander Schmemann, late professor of theology at St. Vladimir's Russian Orthodox Seminary, New York State. *For the Life of the*

World: Sacraments and Orthodoxy (Crestwood, N.Y.: St. Vladimir's Seminary Press, 1974), 97.

James Earl Massey, Dean of Chapel at Tuskegee Institute, Alabama. *Spiritual Disciplines* (Grand Rapids, Mich.: Francis Asbury Press, 1985), 66.

James Earl Massey, *Spiritual Disciplines,* 66.

Dallas Willard, *The Spirit of the Disciplines,* 159.

Gerald May, psychiatrist, director of spiritual guidance at Shalem Institute, Bethesda, Maryland. *Addiction and Grace* (San Francisco: Harper & Row, 1988), 17, 92.

William Ralph Inge, English religious philosopher and churchman, 1860–1954. *Goodness and Truth* (London: Mowbray, 1958), 76–77.

Macrina Wiederkehr, *A Tree Full of Angels,* 36–37.

Dallas Willard, *The Spirit of the Disciplines,* 167.

Chapter 6

M. Scott Peck, psychiatrist, retreat leader, and author. *The Road Less Traveled: A New Psychology of Love, Traditional Values and Spiritual Growth* (New York: Touchstone Books, Simon & Schuster, 1978), 52.

Richard Baxter, a Puritan divine, 1615–1691. *The Saints' Everlasting Rest* 1650, Chap. 8.

Kenneth Leech, Anglican priest, author, and lecturer. *True Prayer: An Invitation to Christian Spirituality* (San Francisco: Harper & Row, 1980), 135.

Ronald V. Wells, minister, professor, and seminar leader. *Spiritual Disciplines for Everyday Living* (Schenectady, N.Y.: Character Research Press, 1982), 97.

Richard Baxter, *The Saints' Everlasting Rest,* Chap. 8.

Richard J. Hauser, Jesuit Professor of Theology, Creighton University. *Moving in the Spirit: Becoming a Contemplative in Action* (New York: Paulist Press, 1986), 55.

In *The Sayings of the Desert Fathers,* The Alphabetical Collection, trans. Benedicta Ward (Kalamazoo, Mich.: Cistercian Publications, 1975), 117.

Chapter 7

Eugene H. Peterson, Professor of Spiritual Theology at Regent College, Vancouver, B.C. *Under the Unpredictable Plant: An Exploration of Vocational Holiness* (Grand Rapids, Mich.: Wm. B. Eerdmans Publishing Co., 1992), 181.

Teresa of Avila, Carmelite nun, monastic reformer, and mystic, 1515–1582. *The Life of Teresa of Jesus: The Autobiography of St. Teresa of Avila,* trans. and ed. E. Allison Peers (Garden City, N.Y.: Doubleday Image Books, 1960), 146.

Tilden Edwards, Director of Shalem Institute for Spiritual Formation, Bethesda, Maryland. *Spiritual Friend: Reclaiming the Gift of Spiritual Direction* (New York: Paulist Press, 1980), 86.

Margaret Guenther, professor of Ascetical Theology and Director of the Center for Christian Spirituality at General Theological Seminary, New York City. *Holy Listening: The Art of Spiritual Direction* (Boston: Cowley Publications, 1992), 43.

Ben Campbell Johnson, Professor of Evangelism and Church Growth, Columbia Theological Seminary, Decatur, Georgia. *To Pray God's Will: Continuing the Journey* (Philadelphia: Westminster Press, 1987), 89.

Ben Campbell Johnson, *To Pray God's Will,* 89.

Tilden Edwards, *Spiritual Friend,* 67.

Kenneth Leech, *True Prayer,* 50.

Dom Columba Marmion, Benedictine Abbot of Meredsous, 1858–1923. Quoted in Kenneth Leech, *Soul Friend: The Practice of Christian Spirituality* (San Francisco: Harper & Row, 1977), 73.

Eugene H. Peterson, *Under the Unpredictable Plant,* 183.

Tilden Edwards, *Spiritual Friend,* 110.

Teresa of Avila, *The Life of Teresa of Jesus,* 144.

Eugene H. Peterson, *Under the Unpredictable Plant,* 186.

Chapter 8

Matthew Fox, iconoclastic Dominican scholar turned Episcopal priest, originator of "Creation Spirituality." *Original Blessing* (Santa Fe, N.M.: Bear & Company, 1983), 112–13.

Todd H. Speidell, contemporary historical theologian, paraphrasing Gregory of Nyssa, Bishop of Nyssa and younger brother of Basil the Great, ca. 330–395. "Incarnational Social Ethics" in *Incarnational Ministry: The Presence of Christ in Church, Society, and Family,* ed. Kettler & Speidell (Colorado Springs: Helmers & Howard Pub., 1990), 140–41.

Karl Barth, Swiss Protestant theologian in Basle, leading theological opponent to Nazism, 1886–1968. *Ethics,* ed. Dietrich Braun, trans. Geoffrey W. Bromiley (New York: Seabury, 1981), 339–40.

Brother Lawrence, *The Practice of the Presence of God,* 82–83.

Todd H. Speidell on Karl Barth, "Incarnational Social Ethics," 147.

Elizabeth Canham, Episcopal priest, Director of Stillpoint Ministries Retreat Center in Black Mountain, North Carolina. "A School for the Lord's Service," in *Weavings* 9, no. 1 (January–February): 13.

Elizabeth Canham, "A School for the Lord's Service," 15.

Parker J. Palmer, Quaker Protestant author and education consultant. *The Company of Strangers: Christians and the Renewal of America's Public Life* (New York: Crossroad, 1986), 145.

Henri J. M. Nouwen, *Reaching Out: The Three Movements of the Spiritual Life* (Garden City, N.Y.: Doubleday & Company, 1975), 60.

Chapter 9

Benedict of Nursia, founder of Benedictine monasticism, 480–547. In Prologue to *The Rule of St. Benedict*, trans. with intro. and notes by Anthony C. Meisel and M. L. del Mastro (Garden City, N.Y.: Doubleday & Company, Image Books, 1975), 45.

William O. Paulsell, former Dean of Lexington Theological Seminary and Disciples of Christ minister. "Ways of Prayer: Designing a Personal Rule of Life," in *Weavings* 2, no. 5 (November–December 1987): 44.

Benedict of Nursia, *The Rule of St. Benedict*, Prologue, 45.

John Wesley, Anglican clergyman, evangelist, and founder of Methodism, 1703–1791. From letter to a lay preacher, cited in Umphrey Lee, *John Wesley and Modern Religion* (Nashville: Cokesbury Press, 1936), 107–08.

Selected Annotated
Bibliography

General Books and Sources
on the Christian Spiritual Life

Boulding, Maria. *The Coming of God*, Collegeville, Minn.: Liturgical Press, 1982.

> A magnificent, deeply heartening book on our hunger for God and how God comes to meet that hunger in us.

Caprio, Betsy, and Thomas M. Hedburg. *Coming Home: A Handbook for Exploring the Sanctuary Within*. Mahwah, N.J.: Paulist Press, 1986.

> A delightfully playful yet in-depth exploration of one's inner journey to God through self-understanding and integration, from a Jungian perspective. Filled with practical exercises and accompanied by evocative, often humorous drawings.

Chaffee, Paul, Judith Favor, William Moreman, Fay Oliver, and Flora Wuellner. *Spirit Awakening: A Book of Practices*. Publication of the Northern California Conference, United Church of Christ, 1988. San Francisco: Word/Press Production.

> A simple introduction to beginning spiritual life practices from a Reformed perspective.

Edwards, Tilden. *Living in the Presence: Disciplines for the Spiritual Heart*. San Francisco: Harper & Row, 1987.

> Truly a book of spiritual life practices, including twenty-seven exercises under themes such as Seeing, Communing, Re-membering, Acting, and Appreciating. Offers a helpful section on spiritual practices in small groups.

Foster, Richard J. *Celebration of Discipline: The Path to Spiritual Growth*. San Francisco: Harper & Row, 1988.

> Still the best, most comprehensive, and most accessible overview of the Christian life and its disciplines. Study guide available.

Gorsuch, John P. *An Invitation to the Spiritual Journey*. Mahwah, N.J.: Paulist Press, 1990.

> A graceful, inviting book on spiritual growth and the practices that lead us toward God.

Johnson, Ben Campbell. *Something More*. Decatur, Ga.: CTS Press, 1993.
   A true beginner's booklet, inviting ordinary people to explore their
   hunger for God.

_____. *To Will God's Will: Beginning the Journey*. Philadelphia:
Westminster Press, 1987.

_____. *To Pray God's Will: Continuing the Journey*. Philadelphia:
Westminster Press, 1987.
   Companion volumes that helpfully introduce readers to the spiritual
   journey, offering concrete pathways into the mystery of God's gracious
   will for us. Include exercises and suggestions for journal keeping.

Kelly, Thomas. *A Testament of Devotion*. New York: Harper & Row,
1941.
   Great modern classic on the Christian spiritual life, by a beloved
   Quaker writer.

Massey, James Earl. *Spiritual Disciplines: Growth through the Practice of
Prayer, Fasting, Dialogue, and Worship*. Grand Rapids: Francis Asbury
Press, 1985.
   A helpful look at the importance of two "hidden" and two "social"
   disciplines.

Nouwen, Henri J. M. *Life of the Beloved: Spiritual Living in a Secular
World*. New York: Crossroad, 1992.
   An effort to catch the ear of secular people who seek spiritual real-
   ity with a word of God's enduring acceptance and love.

_____. *Making All Things New: An Invitation to the Spiritual Life*. San
Francisco: Harper & Row, 1981.
   One of the most prolific and well loved of contemporary spiritual
   writers offers a simple introduction to the meaning of Christian spirituality and how to live it.

_____. *The Way of the Heart: Desert Spirituality and Contemporary
Ministry*. New York: Seabury Press, 1985.
   Drawing on the rich sources of early desert wisdom, Nouwen opens
   out the spiritual treasures of silence, solitude, and prayer.

Ramey, Robert H., and Ben Campbell Johnson. *Living the Christian
Life: A Guide to Reformed Spirituality*. Louisville, Ky.: Westminster
John Knox Press, 1992.
   Treats worship, prayer, scripture, and sacraments in a manner thor-
   oughly rooted in Calvin's piety. Reflection questions for each chap-
   ter, and two good appendices: "Lesson Plans for Group Use," and
   "Guidelines for Spiritual Exercises."

Rice, Howard L. *Reformed Spirituality: An Introduction for Believers*.
Louisville, Ky.: Westminster/John Knox Press, 1991.
   Recovers the riches of Reformed spirituality and its roots in our ear-
   lier Christian heritage. A tonic for Presbyterians, Baptists, Congrega-

tionalists, and Christian Reformed believers in an era of abundant resources from Orthodox, Catholic, Anglican, and Quaker traditions. Study guide available.

Thurman, Howard. *Disciplines of the Spirit.* Richmond, Ind.: Friends United Press, 1963.

> The great Quaker African-American teacher and writer explores themes of commitment, growth, suffering, prayer, and reconciliation in the Christian life. Powerful, incisive, practical, and poetic.

Weavings: A Journal of the Christian Spiritual Life. Nashville: Upper Room.

> The preeminent ecumenical journal of the Christian spiritual life. Each issue explores a particular theme through articles, practical helps, poetry, and book reviews. Published six times a year.

Spiritual Reading

Coupar, Regina. *The Spirit Sings: Reflections from an Artist's Journal.* Truro, Nova Scotia: Gamaliel Publications, 1992.

> A delightful and beautifully produced book of poetic reflections and art that explore central themes of the Christian life. A fine resource for meditation and reflection, especially for those who respond to an artistic medium of expression.

Hall, Thelma. *Too Deep for Words: Rediscovering Lectio Divina.* Mahwah, N.J.: Paulist Press, 1988.

> Excellent overview of *Lectio Divina*, followed by suggested scripture readings organized under several themes. Ideal for spiritual reading with scripture.

Muto, Susan. *Approaching the Sacred: An Introduction to Spiritual Reading.* Denville, N.J.: Dimension Books, 1973.

———. *Steps along the Way: The Path of Spiritual Reading.* Denville, N.J.: Dimension Books, 1975.

> Two early books by the preeminent writer on spiritual reading. An excellent, readable instruction, and a practical guide to this discipline.

Pooley, Roger, and Philip Seddon, eds. *The Lord of the Journey: A Reader in Christian Spirituality.* London: Collins, 1986.

> A superb collection of classic spiritual writings from Orthodox, Evangelical, Catholic, and Ecumenical authors spanning every Christian century. Organized by themes representing basic "life-stages of the Christian pilgrimage." Excellent source for spiritual reading beyond scripture.

Vest, Norvene. *No Moment Too Small: Rhythms of Silence, Prayer, and Holy Reading.* Boston: Cowley Publications, 1994.

> A lovely book on Benedictine spirituality with a substantial chapter

on *Lectio Divina* (holy reading). Readable and applied to daily life. Includes exercises.

Wiederkehr, Macrina. *A Tree Full of Angels: Seeing the Holy in the Ordinary*. HarperSanFrancisco, 1991.

Writing that embodies the fruit of spiritual reading. The author reveals a heart steeped in scripture and the writings of the saints. Helps the reader to awaken to the presence of God. Pure delight.

Prayer

Bergan, Jacqueline, and S. Marie Schwan. *Love: A Guide to Prayer*. Winona, Minn.: St. Mary's Press, 1985.

First of five books in a series called Take and Receive. Themes of the other four guides are: forgiveness, birth, surrender, and freedom. Simple steps, based on Ignatian spiritual exercises, move the reader deeper into committed intimacy with God. Beautifully produced, inviting, and solid.

Bloom, Anthony. *Beginning to Pray*. New York: Paulist Press, 1970.

A modern classic, written by a beloved Russian Orthodox archbishop.

Brooke, Avery. *Learning and Teaching Christian Meditation*. Cambridge, Mass.: Cowley Publications, 1990.

A helpful, readable introduction to various forms of Christian meditation.

_____. *Plain Prayers in a Complicated World*. Boston: Cowley Publications, 1993,

A wonderful collection of honest, unpretentious prayers for virtually every condition and occasion of human life.

Cobb, John B. *Praying for Jennifer: An Exploration of Intercessory Prayer in Story Form*. Nashville: Upper Room, 1985.

Take a journey toward deeper understanding of intercession, in company with committed but perplexed teenagers as they talk with various adults about God, prayer, and their friend Jennifer who remains in a coma after a car accident.

DelBene, Ron, with Mary and Herb Montgomery. *The Breath of Life: A Simple Way to Pray*. Minneapolis: Winston Press, 1981.

_____. *Into the Light: A Simple Way to Pray with the Sick and Dying*. Nashville: Upper Room, 1988.

Two practical books on breath prayer, how to practice it, and ways of praying with family and friends. *Into the Light* is helpful for believing social workers and health care professionals who work with the dying as well as to general readers. Comes with study guide and three booklets for the terminally ill and their loved ones.

de Mello, Anthony. *Sadhana: A Way to God*. Garden City, N.J.: Image Books, 1984.

Practical exercises in awareness, contemplation, imagery, and devotion.

Johnson, Ben Campbell. *Invitation to Pray*. Decatur, Ga.: CTS Press, 1992.

Simple, straightforward guidance into five ways of prayer is the substance of this booklet. Includes leader's guide for group study.

Killinger, John. *Beginning Prayer*. Nashville: Upper Room, 1993.

A simple and practical introduction to a wide variety of methods in prayer.

Brother Lawrence. *The Practice of the Presence of God*. Trans. Robert J. Edmonson. Orleans, Mass.: Paraclete Press, 1985.

A beloved devotional classic on experiencing the presence of God among the pots and pans as well as the solemn choir.

Leech, Kenneth. *True Prayer: An Invitation to Christian Spirituality*. San Francisco: Harper & Row, 1980.

A superb and theologically sound overview of prayer in relation to virtually every aspect of human life.

Merton, Thomas. *New Seeds of Contemplation*. New York: New Directions, 1972.

Perhaps Merton's most accessible yet profound collection of meditations.

Norris, Gunilla. *Being Home: A Book of Meditations*. New York: Bell Tower, 1991.

A magnificently simple and elegant book of meditation on divine presence in the midst of ordinary home activities.

Nouwen, Henri J. M. *Behold the Beauty of the Lord: Praying with Icons*. Notre Dame, Ind.: Ave Maria Press, 1987.

Inspired by the ancient prayer traditions of Eastern Orthodox Christianity, Nouwen guides the reader into a way of prayer unfamiliar to Western Christians. Includes reproductions of four well-known icons (holy images).

_____. *With Open Hands*. Notre Dame, Ind.: Ave Maria Press, 1972.
A modern classic on opening our lives to God in freedom and trust.

Steere, Douglas V. *Dimensions of Prayer*. New York: Women's Division, Board of Global Ministries of the United Methodist Church, 1962.

A modern classic on various aspects of prayer, from one of the eminent voices of the Quaker tradition. Helpful sections on prayer and change, the power of prayer, and prayer and action.

Weatherhead, Leslie D. *The Will of God*. Nashville: Abingdon Press, 1972.

Clear and illuminating approach to one of the most baffling and painful issues of prayer. A genuine help on the subject of God's will.

Wolff, Pierre. *May I Hate God?* New York: Paulist Press, 1979.

When inexplicable tragedy or terror strikes, may we hate God? Wolff, a retreat master, addresses our pain, anguish, and anger in the company of Job and Jesus.

Corporate Worship

Bowyer, O. Richard, Betty Hart, and Charlotte A. Meade, eds. *Prayer in the Black Tradition*. Nashville: Upper Room, 1986.

> The authors describe how central prayer is to the experience of grace in African-American worship.

Foster, Richard J. *Celebration of Discipline: The Path to Spiritual Growth*. Chap. 11: "The Discipline of Worship." San Francisco: Harper & Row, 1988.

> Excellent on worship as a whole. Includes preparation for and fruits of worship.

Massey, James Earl. *Spiritual Disciplines: Growth through the Practice of Prayer, Fasting, Dialogue, and Worship*. Chap. 5: "The Discipline of Worship." Grand Rapids: Francis Asbury Press, 1985.

> Includes an interesting treatment of the role of music in worship.

Ramey, Robert H., and Ben Campbell Johnson. *Living the Christian Life: A Guide to Reformed Spirituality*. Louisville, Ky.: Westminster/John Knox Press, 1992.

> A Reformed perspective on worship, scripture, and sacrament.

Rice, Howard L. *Reformed Spirituality: An Introduction for Beginners*. Chap. 7: "The Discipline of the Christian Life." Louisville, Ky.: Westminster/John Knox Press, 1991.

> Includes sections on worship, sacrament, giving, and Sabbath keeping.

Saliers, Don E. *Worship and Spirituality*. Philadelphia: Westminster Press, 1984.

> A scholar and man of passionate faith helps us reclaim the power of worship to transform our way of perceiving and living in the world.

Personal and Family Worship

Baillie, John. *A Diary of Private Prayer*. New York: Charles Scribner's Sons, 1949.

> A great devotional classic of this century. Morning and evening prayers from a Scottish chaplain, for a month of personal or family worship.

Book of Common Worship: Daily Prayer. Theology and Worship Ministry Unit for the Presbyterian Church (U.S.A.) and the Cumberland Presbyterian Church. Louisville, Ky.: Westminster/John Knox Press, 1993.

Excellent, ecumenically minded resource for personal and group use. Includes morning, evening, midday, and night prayer liturgies; the Psalms in inclusive language for antiphonal reading or singing; a fine collection of prayers for all occasions; and a daily lectionary. Easy to use. Highly recommended.

Edwards, Tilden. *Sabbath Time: Understanding and Practice for Contemporary Christians*. New York: Seabury Press, 1982.

A modern exposition of the nature and need for Sabbath. Edwards treats both the historical practice of Sabbath keeping and ways of preserving the quality of Sabbath time in everyday life.

Hansel, Tim. *When I Relax I Feel Guilty*. Elgin, Ill.: David C. Cook Publishing, 1979.

A good-humored, practical guide for guilt-ridden overachievers. Helpful book on the critical importance of Sabbath-time in life, and how to take it.

Hays, Edward. *Prayers for a Planetary Pilgrim: A Personal Manual for Prayer and Ritual*. Easton, Kans.: Forest of Peace Books, 1988.

Described as "daily prayers for the twenty-first century," this contemporary collection has an interfaith element. Includes morning and evening prayer for all four seasons; psalms, prayers, and rituals for all seasons and occasions; suggestions for gesture and sacred space.

Job, Reuben P., and Norman Shawchuck. *A Guide to Prayer for Ministers and Other Servants*. Nashville: Upper Room, 1983.

Well-received resource by clergy and laity. Provides simple pattern for daily worship, focused on scripture, prayer, and meditation. Structured by weekly themes, each with fine selection of short passages from devotional classics across the centuries. Also twelve models for monthly personal retreats.

_____. *A Guide to Prayer for All God's People*. Nashville: Upper Room, 1990.

Sequel to the above, with same format. New themes, and broader selection of readings from contemporary Christian writers.

Fasting

Foster, Richard J. *Celebration of Discipline: The Path to Spiritual Growth*. Chap. 4: "The Discipline of Fasting." San Francisco: Harper & Row, 1988.

Very useful treatment of a much-neglected topic. Speaks to the theological and spiritual dimensions of fasting. Includes practical matters.

Massey, James Earl. *Spiritual Disciplines: Growth through the Practice of Prayer, Fasting, Dialogue, and Worship*. Chap. 3: "The Discipline of Fasting." Grand Rapids: Francis Asbury Press, 1985.

Primarily a scriptural and historical look at the practice. Includes interesting perspective on what he calls Gandhi's "coercive fasts."

Metz, Johannes B. *Poverty of Spirit.* New York: Paulist Press, 1968.
> A remarkably simple and profound book on the kind of inner "emptiness" that makes us aware of our need to be filled by the life only God can give. Articulates the spiritual reality behind fasting.

Rice, Howard L. "Feasting and Fasting in the Reformed Tradition." *Pacific Theological Review* 22 (fall 1988).
> A helpful review of the biblical and historical roots of fasting, and its importance to Reformed Christians. Explores relationship of feasting and fasting, especially in connection with the Lord's Supper. Suggests practical benefits the recovery of fasting could have for contemporary Christians.

Self-Examination

Douglass, Deborah Smith. "The Examen Re-examined," *Weavings* 10, no. 2 (March–April 1995): 33–40.
> A contemporary writer and poet discovers positive meaning and transforming power in her experience with the Ignatian examination of consciousness.

Foster, Richard J. *Celebration of Discipline: The Path to Spiritual Growth.* Chap. 10: "The Discipline of Confession." San Francisco: Harper & Row, 1988.
> Particularly valuable on subject of confessing to a brother or sister in the faith, and in counsel on giving and receiving confession.

Hauser, Richard J. *Moving in the Spirit: Becoming a Contemplative in Action.* Mahwah, N.J.: Paulist Press, 1987.
> In personal, nontechnical language, a Jesuit priest shares his own practice of spiritual disciplines, including examination of consciousness.

Johnson, Ben Campbell. *To Pray God's Will: Continuing the Journey.* Chap. 3: "Listening to God in the Present Moment." Philadelphia: Westminster Press, 1987.
> Offers a fine introduction to the kind of awareness that prepares us for the simple "way of reflecting on the day" described at the end.

Leech, Kenneth. *True Prayer: An Invitation to Christian Spirituality.* Chap. 5: "Prayer and Penitence." San Francisco: Harper & Row, 1980.
> Includes excellent material on examination of conscience. Offers reader questions for self-examination based on Beatitudes and seven deadly sins.

McIntyre, John P. "Accountability before God: The Examen." In *Spiritual Traditions for the Contemporary Church*, ed. Robin Maas and Gabriel O'Donnell. Nashville: Abingdon Press, 1990.
> A somewhat scholarly but eminently practical description of the Ignatian method of examination of conscience. Leads reader through

preparation and five steps: acknowledging, asking, admitting, repenting, and resolving.

Miller, Keith J. *A Hunger for Healing: The Twelve Steps as a Classical Model for Christian Spiritual Growth*. San Francisco: Harper & Row, 1991.

_____. *A Hunger for Healing Workbook*. San Francisco: Harper & Row, 1992.

> Companion volumes, articulating principles of Christian conversion and spiritual growth in Twelve-Step programs. Steps four and ten have particular application for self-examination, but the whole process is pertinent to ongoing examination of life and conversion of heart.

Rice, Howard L. *Reformed Spirituality: An Introduction for Believers*. Chap. 5: "Consultation: Spiritual Guidance in the Reformed Tradition." Louisville, Ky.: Westminster/John Knox Press, 1991.

> Begins with themes of church discipline and confession, the ground of mutual accountability within the Body of Christ.

Spiritual Guidance

Bankson, Marjory Z. *Seasons of Friendship*. San Diego: LuraMedia, 1987.
> A beautifully written book about the dynamics of friendship, including friendship with God, interpreted through the lens of the biblical story of Naomi and Ruth.

Bonhoeffer, Dietrich. *Life Together*. New York: Harper & Brothers, 1954.
> A modern classic on living together in Christian community with discipline, accountability, and mutual guidance.

Edwards, Tilden. *Spiritual Friend: Reclaiming the Gift of Spiritual Direction*. New York: Paulist Press, 1980.
> The most comprehensive overall introduction to the history and practice of spiritual guidance in print. Scholarly, but readable and practical.

Foster, Richard J. *Celebration of Discipline: The Path to Spiritual Growth*. Chap. 12: "The Discipline of Guidance." San Francisco: Harper & Row, 1988.
> Particularly valuable for perspective on corporate guidance from Quaker tradition.

Guenther, Margaret. *Holy Listening: The Art of Spiritual Direction*. Boston: Cowley Publications, 1992.
> Simply written, yet full of depth and breadth in its practical wisdom. One of the best recent books on the art of spiritual guidance.

Johnson, Ben Campbell. *To Pray God's Will: Continuing the Journey*. Chap. 5: "Spiritual Companionship on the Journey." Philadelphia: Westminster Press, 1987.

Delightfully simple and helpful approach, from shared personal journey.

Kelsey, Morton T. *Companions on the Inner Way: The Art of Spiritual Guidance*. New York: Crossroad, 1984.

Demanding reading, but rich with personal story, psychological and spiritual insight. Written from a Jungian perspective.

Leech, Kenneth. *Soul Friend: The Practice of Christian Spirituality*. New York: Harper & Row, 1977.

The definitive historical handbook on the nature and varieties of spiritual direction in every major Christian tradition.

Peterson, Eugene H. *Under the Unpredictable Plant: An Exploration in Vocational Holiness*. Chap. 5: "Quarreling with God under the Unpredictable Plant." Grand Rapids: Wm. B. Eerdmans Publishing Co., 1992.

Addresses the pastoral role of spiritual direction through personal stories and theological reflection. Incisive, graceful style.

Rice, Howard L. *Reformed Spirituality: An Introduction for Believers*. Chap. 5: "Consultation: Spiritual Guidance in the Reformed Tradition." Louisville, Ky.: Westminster/John Knox Press, 1991.

Useful guidelines for those seeking guidance and those considering offering it.

Hospitality

Hawkins, Thomas R. *Sharing the Search: A Theology of Christian Hospitality*. Nashville: Upper Room, 1987.

A readable and substantive book on the centrality of hospitality in Christian life.

Koenig, John. *New Testament Hospitality*. Philadelphia: Fortress Press, 1985.

Scholarly but accessible book that covers historical and theological perspectives on Christian hospitality.

Nouwen, Henri J. M. *Reaching Out: The Three Movements of the Spiritual Life*. Garden City, N.Y.: Doubleday & Co., 1975.

One of Nouwen's earlier classics. Treats movement from hostility to hospitality at home, in the classroom, and in pastoral care.

Palmer, Parker J. *The Company of Strangers: Christians and the Renewal of America's Public Life*. New York: Crossroad, 1986.

Refreshing treatment of public life and the vital role of strangers in a healthy community. Eye-opening on the nature of genuine hospitality.

_____. *To Know as We Are Known: A Spirituality of Education*. San Francisco: Harper & Row, 1983.

Entire book is an eloquent argument for a truly hospitable way of teaching.

Weavings 9, no. 1 (January–February 1994).

Entire issue is devoted to exploring the theme of hospitality; articles, poems, and book reviews, including Koenig's *New Testament Hospitality* (see Koenig, above).

Rule of Life

Paulsell, William O. *Rules for Prayer.* Mahwah, N.J.: Paulist Press, 1993.

Drawing on writings of saints through the centuries, Paulsell introduces a wide range of rules of life and prayer. One of the few books of its kind. Helpful background for developing one's own rule of life.

Rule of St. Benedict, The. Translated, with introduction and notes, by Anthony C. Meisel and M. L. del Mastro. Garden City, N.Y.: Doubleday & Company, Image Books, 1975.

Classic sixth-century rule of life designed by Benedict of Nursia for well-being and peace of monastic community. Its practical wisdom continues to nourish and inspire both monks and laypersons.